INSPIRING STORIES
FOR
AMAZING KIDS

*Motivational Tales of Courage,
Kindness, Confidence, and
Believing in Your Dreams*

2 IN 1

Katie Wensley

Contents

INSPIRING STORIES FOR AMAZING GIRLS

Introduction 1

Beyond the Comfort Zone 2

The Paws of Kindness.................................... 11

United We Rise 17

Courage on Wheels 26

The Science of Truth 34

Heritage and Heart.. 43

Stand Tall 51

Facing the Fear 60

The Power of Pause 67

Changing Her Tune 74

Conclusion 81

Contents

INSPIRING STORIES
FOR
AMAZING BOYS

Introduction 1

The Not-So-Superhero.................................... 2

The Reckless Racer 9

The Littlest Explorer 18

The Jealous Friend.................................... 25

The Careless Student 32

The Recipe Book 40

The Lonely Bully 47

The Shelter Helpers.................................... 54

The Unkind Leader 61

The Video Game Glitch.................................. 69

Conclusion... 75

INSPIRING STORIES
FOR
AMAZING GIRLS

Empowering Tales of Courage,
Confidence, and Kindness

Katie Wensley

Introduction

Do you ever feel like life is a tornado that sweeps you off your feet, leaving you unsure how to find solid ground again? At times, it's amazing! Sometimes, it's disappointing. And every so often, it's scary. You're not alone in this world, and there are so many other girls like you who are feeling exactly the way you are right now.

Join me in a world where dreams take flight, friendships blossom in the most unexpected places, and young girls like you discover the power that lies within. Each story in this book is a reminder that no matter where you come from or what you face, you have the strength, creativity, and determination to shape your own future.

You'll meet girls who overcame their fears, stood up for what they believed in, learned the value of kindness, discovered new talents, made lasting friendships, and came to cherish the qualities that make them unique. These aren't just stories of triumph; they are tales of growth, bravery, and the magic that unfolds when you believe in yourself.

As you turn the pages, you may see a bit of yourself in each of these characters, and that's a wonderful thing. I hope you find the inspiration to chase your dreams with passion, face obstacles with courage, and always, always believe in the power of being yourself.

Beyond the Comfort Zone

The sun rose over the quiet suburban neighborhood where Aaliyah Dembay lived. Aaliyah, a 10-year-old girl with wide brown eyes and curly dark brown hair—she got her hair from her father—that framed her light brown face, lay in bed, staring at the ceiling.

Aaliyah loved being outdoors, but today she was feeling off. For years, she'd been swimming and hiking with her family and playing baseball with her friends, yet her heart felt restless.

As Aaliyah dressed in her favorite yellow sundress, she thought about the things she loved—like reading books where the good guys always won, doing jigsaw puzzles with her mom, and watching movies with happy endings. She was always drawn to simple and pure stories in which kindness and goodness triumphed. Lately, even those things didn't seem to fill the space inside her that longed for something new.

The smell of pancakes filled the air, so she bounded downstairs. Aaliyah's mother Krista flipped the golden-brown treats onto a plate. Her father, Tyrese, poured orange juice, and her older brother Josiah, who was 12, was already seated at the table eating.

"Morning, sweet pea," Krista said. She smiled as Aaliyah entered the kitchen.

"Morning, Mom," Aaliyah replied, sliding into her seat across from Josiah. She loved her mom's golden hair, light green eyes, and, most of all, her cheerful nature.

"What's wrong, Aaliyah? You've been quiet lately," Tyrese observed as he sat beside her.

Aaliyah shrugged, poking at her pancake. "I don't know, Dad. I guess I'm just bored."

Josiah snickered. "Bored? How can you be bored when there's baseball to play?"

Aaliyah sighed. "I like swimming and baseball, but it feels like I've been doing the same things forever. I want to try something different."

"Like what?" Krista asked.

Aaliyah hesitated. "Martial arts."

Josiah burst out laughing, nearly choking on his juice. "Martial arts? That's for boys, Aaliyah! You'd get crushed! You're just copying me because I take martial arts!"

"No, I'm not!" Aaliyah replied. She was telling the truth. This had nothing to do with her brother.

Aaliyah's cheeks flushed with embarrassment. She wasn't strong like Josiah, and the idea of stepping into a martial arts class with many boys scared her. But there was also something exciting about it.

"Josiah, that's enough," Tyrese said firmly, giving his son a stern look. "Martial arts isn't just for boys."

"But Dad, I don't want her taking Martial arts with me—" Josiah began, but Krista cut him off.

Josiah didn't argue any further. Aaliyah looked at her parents, feeling hopeful, but the knot of anxiety in her stomach remained. What if Josiah was right? What if she wasn't any good at it?

"Josiah, your sister can try whatever she wants." Krista smiled warmly, brushing a stray curl from Aaliyah's forehead. "You can do anything you set your mind to, sweetie. If you want to learn martial arts, then we'll support you all the way. Just remember, it's not about being the best right away- it's about trying, learning, and growing."

Aaliyah glared at her brother and said, "What if Josiah's right?"

Tyrese reached across the table and took her hand in his. "The only way to find out is to try. No matter what happens, we're proud of you for having the courage to try something new."

Later that day, Aaliyah met up with her best friend Zara at the park. Zara had long, dark hair and an adventurous spirit that always inspired Aaliyah. They found a quiet spot under a tree, where they often sat to talk about everything.

"What's wrong, Aaliyah?" Zara asked, leaning against a tree.

Aaliyah bit her lip, unsure of how to start. But Zara had always been her friend, so she took a deep breath and let the words spill out.

"I've been thinking about trying martial arts," Aaliyah admitted, twisting a strand of her hair nervously. "But I'm scared I won't be any good at it. And Josiah says it's only for boys."

Zara's eyes lit with excitement. "You'd be great at martial arts! Don't listen to Josiah—he's just trying to mess with you."

Aaliyah smiled weakly. "Maybe, but I'm not strong or coordinated. What if they laugh at me?"

Zara shook her head. "Aaliyah, you've always been good at everything you try. You're smart, you're quick, and you've got a big heart. Those are the things that matter. Besides, everyone starts somewhere, right? You don't have to be perfect from the start."

Aaliyah looked down, still uncertain. "I don't know, Zara. I just wish I could be sure that I'd be good at it before I even start."

Zara squeezed Aaliyah's hand. "The only way to find out is to try. And I'll be there to cheer you on."

Aaliyah felt a spark of courage flicker inside. Zara was right. She couldn't let fear hold her back from trying something new. But the thought of *actually* walking into a martial arts studio still made her heart race with anxiety.

That evening, as Aaliyah closed her eyes, she imagined herself as a martial artist, moving with confidence and skill, just like the people she'd seen on TV.

The next day, while Aaliyah walked home after school, her thoughts swirled with everything her parents said the morning before. As she approached the martial arts studio, her steps slowed, and she found herself peering through the large glass windows with curiosity and fear.

Inside, she saw a group of boys her age practicing their moves with serious expressions. They moved with precision, their kicks and punches sharp and controlled. Aaliyah's heart sank; they all seemed so sure of themselves, so strong.

But then, out of the corner of her eye, she spotted someone different. It was a girl about the same age as Aaliyah, with a confident stance and a determined look in her eyes. She was moving just as skillfully as the boys, her movements fluid and precise.

"Wow," she murmured to herself, feeling admiration and anxiety. *Maybe she was just born talented*, Aaliyah suddenly thought, the flicker of hope starting to dim. She sighed and continued her walk home, the image of the confident girl both inspiring and intimidating her.

The next afternoon, as Aaliyah walked past the martial arts studio again, she noticed the same girl—she recognized her from school and thought her name was Emma—practicing inside. This time, Emma caught Aaliyah's gaze, smiled, and waved her over. Aaliyah hesitated. Her heart raced, but something about Emma's friendly smile made her take a step closer.

"Hi, I'm Emma," the girl said as she stepped outside. "I've seen you at school! Are you thinking about joining?"

Aaliyah shifted on her feet, feeling nervous under Emma's kind but curious gaze. "I want to, but my brother says martial arts is only for boys, and I'm not sure if I'll be any good."

Emma's smile widened. "That's nonsense! Martial arts is for everyone. I was terrified the first time I came here, but once I gave it a try, I realized how much I loved it."

Josiah saw Aaliyah on the way to his martial arts lesson. He approached her and frowned when he saw Aaliyah talking to Emma. "Aaliyah, are you really thinking about this? It'll be too hard. I don't think it's your thing."

Emma crossed her arms and gave Josiah a determined look. "And why not? Aaliyah can do anything she puts her mind to, just like anyone else. In fact, I bet she'd be amazing at martial arts."

Josiah looked between the two girls and sighed. "Fine. But don't say I didn't warn you." He walked away snickering.

Emma turned back to Aaliyah, and her bright blue eyes lit with encouragement. "You'll be great, Aaliyah. Don't let anyone tell you otherwise. I'll be there with you, okay?"

Aaliyah smiled. "Okay. I'll give it a try."

The next day after school, Aaliyah stood in front of the martial arts studio with her heart pounding in her chest. She could hear the muffled sounds of practice inside—shouts, thuds, and the rhythmic stomp of feet on the mat. Taking a deep breath, she pushed the door open and stepped inside.

Emma greeted her with a wide grin. "You made it!"

Aaliyah nodded, her stomach doing flip-flops. "I'm ready."

"I'm Mr. Zhiyu Chien, your sensei. I'm glad you're here. Don't be nervous; just do your best," the instructor said as he greeted her.

Aaliyah took her place on the mat, trying to mirror the stances of the other students. As the class began, she felt the initial awkwardness of her movements, but with each passing minute, she grew more focused and tried to follow Mr. Chien's instructions as closely as possible.

As the class progressed, Aaliyah caught on quicker than expected. Her punches grew more precise, her kicks stronger, and a rhythm developed in her movements. To her surprise it felt natural, almost like she'd been doing it for years.

Mr. Chien gave her an encouraging nod. "Very good, Aaliyah. You're picking this up quickly. Keep it up!"

Emma flashed her a thumbs-up from across the room, and Aaliyah couldn't help but smile. The nervousness that had been sitting in her stomach all day slowly melted away, replaced by a growing sense of confidence. She was doing it—she was actually *doing* it. She couldn't wait to tell her parents!

Over the next few weeks, Aaliyah continued to attend her martial arts classes. She no longer felt out of place among the other students; instead, she felt like she belonged. The moves that once seemed difficult were becoming second nature, and she found herself looking forward to each class more and more. Aaliyah felt a familiar buzz of excitement every time she stepped onto the mat in the martial arts dojo.

One day, as Aaliyah progressed through her martial arts routine, she noticed her form was sharper and more precise. She was no longer hesitant or second-guessing herself. Aaliyah realized that she was getting better. It wasn't just about the kicks and punches; it was the confidence growing inside her.

At the end of their lessons, all the students from each class sat on the mat to listen to Mr. Chien's feedback. Aaliyah couldn't help but feel proud when he called her out.

"Aaliyah," Mr. Chien began, "Your progress is remarkable. You've shown great discipline and focus. Keep up the good work."

Aaliyah's heart swelled with pride. She glanced over at Josiah, who was seated at the far edge of the mat. For a moment, their eyes met, and she saw something in his expression that surprised her—pride. But there was also something else that looked a lot like guilt.

After class Aaliyah and Josiah walked home together. Josiah was unusually quiet. Aaliyah couldn't help but wonder what was going on in his mind. Finally, as they reached the park near their house, Josiah stopped and turned to face her.

"Aaliyah," he started, his voice hesitant. "I want to say I'm sorry."

Aaliyah blinked in surprise. "Sorry? For what?"

Josiah looked down, kicking a pebble on the ground. "For what I said before. About martial arts being just for boys. I was wrong."

Aaliyah stared at him, shocked.

"I heard Mr. Chien praising you today," Josiah admitted. "You're really good—way better than I thought you'd be. I just didn't want to admit that my little sister could be better than me."

Aaliyah felt a lump in her throat. "Josiah, it's okay."

"It's not okay," Josiah insisted. "You're amazing at this. I should have supported you from the start. I'm proud of you and want you to keep going, no matter what."

Aaliyah smiled, her heart feeling happy. "Thanks, Josiah. That means a lot."

He grinned at her. "So are you gonna show me how to do some of those moves?"

Aaliyah laughed. "If you can keep up!"

They raced each other home.

That night, as Aaliyah lay in bed, she thought about everything that had happened. She had started martial arts on a whim, not really knowing what to expect. She had been nervous and unsure if she would even like it, let alone be any good at it. But now, she couldn't imagine her life without it. The thrill of learning something new, the satisfaction of getting better, and the pride she felt in herself were all more than she had ever expected.

Aaliyah realized that stepping out of her comfort zone had led her to discover something wonderful—not just a new skill but a new passion. And she now had a new friend in Emma, one of the popular girls at her school.

Aaliyah was no longer the shy girl who doubted herself at every turn. She had learned that she could be strong, that she could excel at something if she put her mind to it, and, more importantly, that gender didn't determine what she could achieve.

> *Aaliyah's story shows the power of stepping out of your comfort zone. She overcame her doubts and fears and discovered a new passion for martial arts. Aaliyah learned that trying something new can lead to unexpected joy and self-confidence. This teaches us that we can achieve anything if we're willing to take a chance, regardless of others' opinions.*

The Paws of Kindness

Shellene Moffatt stared out the window of her room, watching the rain fall. She sighed, feeling the familiar pang of loneliness, and played with a strand of her short, naturally blond hair. At nine years old, Shellene often felt like a misfit. Adopted and an only child, she struggled to connect with others her age. Her parents, loving and supportive as they were, couldn't quite fill the void she felt inside.

Shellene spotted a tiny, shivering kitten huddled under a bush in their front yard as she looked out the window. Her heart went out to the little creature.

She dashed outside with an umbrella, scooped up the kitten, and rushed back into the house. The kitten was soaking wet, its fur matted and dirty, but it was the most beautiful thing Shellene had ever seen.

"Mom! Dad! Look what I found!" Shellene called out, cradling the kitten in her arms.

Her parents, Donna and Greg, hurried into the living room. Donna's eyes widened at the sight of the disheveled kitten. "Oh, Shellene, you found a stray!"

"We need to take care of it," Shellene insisted, her bright blue eyes pleading.

Greg smiled gently. "All right, let's get it cleaned up first."

Together, they bathed the kitten, who turned out to be a delicate Siamese with striking blue eyes. Shellene named it Smudge and immediately felt a connection she'd never experienced before. Smudge seemed to sense her need for companionship, curling up on her lap and purring contentedly.

The next few days were some of the happiest Shellene had ever known. Smudge became her constant companion, sleeping beside her at night and following her around during the day. She no longer felt so alone. But as much as she loved Smudge, she knew deep down that the kitten might belong to someone else.

One evening, as they sat around the dinner table, Donna brought up the subject that Shellene had been dreading. "Sweetheart, we need to find out if Smudge belongs to someone. It's the right thing to do."

Shellene's heart sank. "But what if no one claims her?"

"Then we can keep her," Greg reassured her. "But we have to try."

Reluctantly, Shellene agreed. The next day, Donna helped her make signs. They printed pictures of Smudge and wrote, "Found Kitten: Siamese, very friendly. Please call if she belongs to you." Together, they put up the signs around the neighborhood. Shellene secretly hoped no one would call.

Shellene's heart would race each time the phone rang, as she feared the call was someone claiming Smudge. But the days went by and no one called about the cat. Shellene started to feel a glimmer of hope that maybe Smudge would stay with her forever.

Time passed, and Smudge became a part of the family. Shellene's parents even bought a small leash, and Shellene started taking Smudge out for little walks up and down the street. On one of these walks, she ran into their elderly neighbor, Elva Novak.

Elva, a kind woman with silver hair and warm eyes, smiled as she saw Shellene and the kitten. "What a beautiful kitten you have there, Shellene."

"Thank you, Mrs. Novak," Shellene replied, beaming. "Her name is Smudge."

Elva's smile faltered slightly. "She looks just like my kitten. I lost her a few weeks ago."

Shellene's heart sank. "Is she a Siamese?"

Elva nodded. "Yes, she is. Her name is Misty. I got her to keep me company after my husband passed away six months ago."

Tears welled up in Shellene's eyes as she realized what she had to do. "I think Smudge might be Misty. I found her a few weeks ago in my yard."

Elva looked at Shellene with a mixture of sadness and gratitude. "Oh, Shellene, thank you for taking such good care of her."

Reluctantly, Shellene handed the leash to Elva. "Here, Mrs. Novak. You should have her back."

Elva took the leash, her eyes misting over. "Oh my goodness, you are such a kind girl, Shellene. I really appreciate you finding my kitten and keeping her safe. You can come visit Misty anytime you want."

Shellene nodded, feeling a lump in her throat. She watched as Elva walked away with the kitten, feeling an ache in her heart. But she knew she had done the right thing.

The next day, Shellene knocked on Elva's door. The older woman answered with a warm smile. "Hello, Shellene. Come in."

Shellene followed Elva into the house, where Misty—formerly Smudge—was lounging comfortably on the couch. The kitten looked up and purred at the sight of Shellene. After petting Misty for awhile, Shellene looked up happily at Elva. Elva noticed the joy in Shellene's eyes and said, "Would you like to help me in the garden?"

Shellene nodded eagerly. She followed Elva outside, and they spent the afternoon tending to the flowers and vegetables. Shellene found that she loved gardening, and even more, she enjoyed spending time with Elva. They talked about everything—from Elva's late husband to Shellene's school life. For the first time in a long while, Shellene felt a sense of belonging.

Days turned into weeks, and Shellene's visits to Elva became a regular occurrence. She helped with the gardening, played with Misty, and listened to Elva's stories. In return, Elva taught her about plants and flowers, sharing her wisdom and experience. Shellene realized that not only did she gain a new friend in Elva, but she also found a passion for gardening.

One sunny afternoon, as they were planting marigolds, Elva looked at Shellene and said, "You know, dear, kindness can change the world."

Shellene paused, thinking about Elva's words. "What do you mean?"

Elva smiled. "If you hadn't been kind enough to give Misty back, we wouldn't have become friends. You've brought so much joy into my life, Shellene. Sometimes, small acts of kindness can make a big difference."

Shellene smiled, feeling a warmth in her heart. She realized that even though she didn't have her own kitten anymore, she had gained something even more precious—a friend and a sense of purpose. She no longer felt like a misfit. She had found her place in the world, and it was filled with kindness and love.

From that day on, Shellene made it her mission to spread kindness wherever she went. She volunteered at the local animal shelter, helped her neighbors with their gardens, and always looked out for those who needed a friend. Through it all, she remembered Elva's words, knowing that her small acts of kindness could indeed change the world.

Shellene's parents watched with pride as their daughter blossomed. Donna often joined Shellene on her visits to Elva's, and they would all share tea and stories together. Greg would sometimes come along too, bringing homemade cookies or lending a hand with heavier gardening tasks. The bond between the Moffatts and Elva grew strong, creating a little close-knit community that supported one another.

One particularly memorable day, Shellene and Elva decided to organize a neighborhood garden party. They had spent weeks preparing, inviting neighbors and friends and decorating Elva's garden with colorful flowers and fairy lights. On the day of the party, the garden was a magical sight, with vibrant blooms and the scent of fresh flowers filling the air.

Neighbors arrived with dishes to share, and the garden buzzed with laughter and conversation. Shellene moved through the crowd, greeting everyone with a smile and feeling a sense of accomplishment and happiness she had never known before. Misty, who wore a little flower crown Shellene had made, pranced around, charming all the guests.

As the sun began to set, Shellene found herself sitting with Elva on a cozy bench in the garden, watching the fairy lights twinkle. Elva patted Shellene's hand and said, "You've brought so much light into this garden and into my life, Shellene. I'm so grateful for you."

Tears of joy filled Shellene's eyes. "I'm grateful for you too, Mrs. Novak. You've taught me so much and made me feel like I belong."

Elva hugged Shellene tightly. "You do belong, my dear. You belong right here where kindness grows."

In the months and years that followed, Shellene continued to nurture her love for gardening and her commitment to kindness. She grew into a compassionate young woman, always ready to lend a helping hand and spread joy wherever she went. And every time she visited Elva, they would sit together in the garden, surrounded by the beauty they had created together, knowing that their friendship was a testament to the power of kindness.

Shellene's story shows that small acts of kindness can create powerful connections. By returning the lost kitten, Shellene found a lifelong friend in her elderly neighbor, Elva. Through this bond, she discovered a sense of belonging and purpose. This teaches us that kindness not only helps others but also brings unexpected joy and fulfillment into our own lives.

United We Rise

Kiana Nakamura loved the way the volleyball felt as it hit her hands, and the satisfying smack that echoed across the gym. Volleyball was more than just a sport to her- it was where she felt strong, confident, and connected to her friends. Since moving to Burlington, Vermont, six years ago from Hawaii, volleyball had become her anchor. It was a place where she could truly be herself.

Lately, Kiana's team had been struggling. After a series of tough matches, their spirits were at an all-time low. Kiana's best friend, Tamara, usually the vibrant spark of the group, had begun to lose some of her shine. Cora, the tallest girl on the team with her long blond hair and gray eyes, was the biggest worrier of them all. If there was something to be anxious about, Cora found it.

One evening after practice, Kiana flopped onto the couch at home, pulling her long black hair out of its usual ponytail and feeling the weight of her team's frustration. Her mom, Mikala, noticed immediately.

"What's wrong, sweetheart?" Mikala asked, sitting down beside her daughter.

Kiana sighed and hugged a throw pillow. "The team's not doing so well, Mom. We're losing matches, and everyone's starting to give up. Even Tamara is losing her confidence, and Cora, well, she's Cora. She's always worrying about everything."

Mikala gently squeezed Kiana's shoulder. "That sounds tough. But I know you, Kiana. You're a natural leader. What do you think needs to change?"

Kiana thought for a moment, chewing on her bottom lip. "I think we need to boost our morale, but I don't know how. I don't know where to start."

Just then, Kiana's dad, Hale, walked into the room. He had overheard the conversation and joined them, sitting on the edge of the coffee table across from Kiana.

"I used to play many sports when I was your age," Hale began, a smile playing at the corners of his mouth. "When my team was in a slump, we didn't give up. We found ways to lift each other up and work through it together."

Kiana perked up, listening intently. "What did you do, Dad?"

Hale leaned in and shared his wisdom. "First, we celebrated small wins. Even if it was just one good play in a match, we'd make a big deal out of it. We also did team bonding activities that didn't involve the sport we were playing— just to build trust and get to know each other better."

Kiana nodded, absorbing every word. "What else?"

"We gave each other constructive feedback. It's important to be honest but also kind. We set clear goals, both as individuals and as a team. We made sure everyone knew their strengths and how they could contribute."

Mikala chimed in, "And remember, recognizing effort is just as important as results. Celebrate how hard everyone is working, not just the wins."

Hale added, "Encourage communication. Make sure everyone feels heard. Sometimes, a pep talk or a good cheer can go a long way. But most importantly, foster a culture of respect and trust. You can't win if you don't trust your teammates."

Kiana's mind was racing with ideas. "That's it! I know what I need to do. Thanks, Mom and Dad!"

The next day at practice, Kiana gathered the team together before they hit the court.

"Hey, everyone," Kiana started, her voice strong and confident. "I know things have been tough lately, but I believe in us. We're a great team, and I think we just need a little boost to get back on track."

Tamara, who was usually brimming with energy, looked up, curious. "What do you have in mind, Kiana?"

Kiana smiled. "I talked to my dad, and he gave me some ideas. What if we start by celebrating our small wins? Like, every time we make a good play, we hype it up. And I think we should do some team bonding activities—something that will help us trust each other—trust falls or other fun exercises that aren't about volleyball."

Cora, who had been quietly listening, frowned slightly. "But what if we mess up? What if it doesn't work?"

Kiana walked over to Cora and placed a reassuring hand on her shoulder. "That's exactly why we need to do this. We have to focus on what we're doing right, not what could go wrong. We're in this together."

Tamara nodded enthusiastically, her energy slowly returning. "I'm in. Let's do this!"

The team agreed, and Kiana suggested they add another weekly practice dedicated solely to teamwork and trust-building. It wasn't just about volleyball anymore; it was about rebuilding their bond as a team.

During their first teamwork practice, Kiana explained one of the exercises: "Okay, for this one, we're going to do trust falls. You stand in front of someone, back-to-front, and then the person in the front falls backward, trusting that your partner will catch you. It's all about trust."

Cora's eyes widened. "What if they don't catch me?"

Tamara, standing next to Cora, grinned. "That's the point. We have to trust each other."

Despite Cora's initial hesitation, she eventually paired up with Tamara, who was quick to offer her infectious smile.

"You got this, Cora. I won't let you fall," Tamara reassured her.

Slowly, Cora leaned back, body stiff with fear, and then she let herself fall. Just as she was about to panic, Tamara caught her, steady and strong. Cora let out a breath she didn't realize she was holding and smiled.

"See? We're in this together," Tamara said, her voice warm.

As the weeks passed, the team continued their special practices, focusing on stamina, agility, and their bond. They ran laps for endurance and did agility drills, box jumps, planks, and lunge twists. Every time someone completed a drill, the others would cheer them on, their voices echoing in the gym, filling it with a new sense of determination.

Kiana could see the difference. Tamara's energy was back and brighter than ever. Cora, while still prone to worry, was starting to smile more as her confidence slowly grew. The entire team felt more connected, more like a family.

Then it happened. The team faced their next match with a new resolve. They communicated better on the court, trusted each other's moves, and celebrated every point, no matter how small. It wasn't just about winning; it was about playing together as one unit.

After a particularly intense rally, Kiana made a perfect set, and Tamara spiked the ball with all her might. The ball hit the ground on the opponent's side, earning Kiana's team the final point in the match.

The gym erupted in cheers. The team hugged each other, laughing and celebrating their hard-fought victory. For the first match in a long time, they felt like a real team again.

That evening, Kiana invited Tamara and Cora over to her house to celebrate. As they walked through the door, Kiana's parents greeted them with warm smiles.

"So, how's the team doing?" Mikala asked, handing them glasses of lemonade.

Kiana beamed, her eyes sparkling with pride. "We won! But it's more than that, Mom. We've been working on our teamwork, just like Dad said. We added an extra weekly practice just to focus on trust and communication. It's really made a difference."

Tamara, her smile as bright as ever, chimed in, "Yeah, we even did trust falls! And Cora, who was super nervous about it at first, totally rocked it!"

Cora blushed, but her smile had a hint of pride. "It was actually kind of fun. And it helped me realize that maybe things won't always go wrong."

Hale, who had been listening quietly, nodded approvingly. "That's great to hear, girls. I'm really proud of you for sticking together and finding a way to lift each other up. That's what being a team is all about."

Mikala added, "And remember, the work doesn't stop here. Keep supporting each other, and you'll continue to grow stronger as a team."

Kiana looked at her parents, her heart swelling with gratitude. "Thanks, Mom. Thanks, Dad. We couldn't have done it without you."

As the season progressed, the team continued to improve. They won match after match, each victory sweeter than the last. They didn't win every game, but when they lost they didn't lose hope. They stuck together as a team. And when they finally made it to the finals of the tournament, they were ecstatic. They had worked hard, not just on their skills, but on their bond as a team.

The day of the finals arrived, and the team huddled together before the match, nerves buzzing with anticipation.

Kiana looked around at her teammates, feeling a surge of pride. "No matter what happens out there today, I'm proud of us. We've come so far, and we've done it together."

Tamara grinned, and her infectious energy lit up the group. "Let's do this, team!"

Cora, her voice steady and confident, added, "Yeah, let's show them what we're made of."

The match was intense, with both teams fighting hard for every point. But Kiana's team was different now. They trusted each other, communicated well, and celebrated every small victory along the way.

When the final whistle blew, they had won. They had achieved the ultimate victory.

A few weeks after their victory, Kiana received an unexpected call from their coach, Mr. Reynolds, who asked to meet her at the gym. When she arrived, he looked more serious than usual.

"Kiana, I've just been informed that our team has been selected to compete in an out-of-state tournament next month," Mr. Reynolds said. "It's a huge opportunity, but there's a catch. We'll be facing some of the best teams in the country, and we're going to need to up our game if we want to stand a chance."

Kiana felt excited and anxious. "Do you think we're ready for this?"

Mr. Reynolds gave her a knowing smile. "I think with the right preparation, you can be. But it's going to require a lot of hard work, and I'm going to need you to help keep the team motivated."

Kiana nodded, determined. "We're up for the challenge, Coach."

One afternoon, Kiana returned home from practice to find her older cousin, Keoni, waiting for her in the living room. Keoni now lived nearby but had been a star volleyball player back in Hawaii, and he was someone Kiana had always looked up to.

"Kiana! Look at you, all grown up and leading your team to victory!" Keoni exclaimed, pulling her into a bear hug.

Kiana laughed, surprised and delighted to see him. "Keoni! What are you doing here?"

Keoni grinned. "I heard about your upcoming tournament, and I thought I'd come by and give you some pointers. I know how much this means to you."

Over the next few days, Keoni helped Kiana and the team refine their skills, sharing tips and techniques that helped him in his own career. His presence gave Kiana a renewed sense of confidence and motivation.

The night before they left for the tournament, Kiana invited the team over to her house for a pre-tournament dinner. Mikala and Hale prepared a feast, and the team sat together, sharing stories and laughing. The nervous energy from earlier in the week melted away.

As they finished dessert, Hale stood up, holding a glass of sparkling cider. "I just want to say how proud I am of all of you. You've worked hard to get here, and no matter what happens tomorrow, you should be proud of yourselves too. Remember, it's not just about winning—it's about playing with heart and supporting each other."

Kiana raised her glass, her voice strong and clear. "To us. To teamwork, to friendship, and to giving it our all tomorrow."

The team clinked their glasses together with their spirits high.

The tournament was tougher than any match they'd faced before. The opposing teams were skilled, and the competition was fierce. Kiana's team struggled in the first game, their nerves getting the better of them.

During a timeout, Kiana gathered them together. "Listen, we didn't come this far to give up now. We know what we're capable of, and we've faced tough challenges before. Let's show them what we're made of!"

The team rallied, and as they stepped back onto the court, their energy shifted. They played with everything they had, trusting each other's abilities and cheering each other on with every point.

Though the final game was close, they ultimately lost by just a few points. But as they gathered together, sweaty and exhausted, Kiana realized that they'd won something much more important—a deeper bond and a sense of pride in how far they'd come.

As they left the court, the team huddled together one last time, their heads held high.

"We may not have won the tournament," Kiana said, "but we've won as a team. And that's something no one can take away from us."

Kiana learned that true strength in a team comes from trust, communication, and celebrating small victories. By focusing on building morale and supporting one another, Kiana and her volleyball team rediscovered their confidence and bond, and it led to greater success. This story reminds us that unity and perseverance can overcome challenges and make every effort count, win or lose.

Courage on Wheels

Sofia Russo's sneakers squeaked against the shiny linoleum floor of the school hallway as she practically skipped toward the cafeteria. Her long chestnut-brown hair bounced behind her in a neat ponytail, and her dark brown eyes sparkled with excitement. Today Mrs. Ransen announced that the sign-up sheet for the school talent show would be posted soon, and Sofia couldn't wait to tell her best friend, Lucy Blackwood.

As Sofia rounded the corner, she spotted Lucy by their usual lunch table. Lucy's blond hair was naturally wavy and sat on her shoulders. Her bright blue eyes, normally filled with mischief, seemed unusually dull. It wasn't like Lucy to look so serious, and Sofia's heart sank as she approached.

"Hey, Luce!" Sofia greeted her cheerfully as she plopped on the bench beside Lucy. "Did you hear? The talent show sign-up sheet is going up soon! Are you going to enter?"

Lucy looked up, a small smile playing on her lips, but it didn't reach her eyes. "I don't know if I'm going to sign up this year, Sof."

Sofia blinked in surprise. "What? But you love performing! Why wouldn't you sign up?"

Lucy shrugged. "Because all anyone will see is this." She gestured to her wheelchair with a resigned sigh. "No one will even pay attention to what I'm doing. They'll just see the girl in the wheelchair and nothing else."

Sofia frowned. "That's not true, Lucy. You're funny, you're smart, and you've got so much talent! You can do anything you want. You did your baton routine last year, didn't you?" She looked at Lucy's wheelchair. "I'm such a bad friend. I got so caught up in the excitement that I forgot that this time last year was before the car accident and you weren't in a wheelchair. I'm so sorry! Maybe you can't do your baton routine, but there's definitely something else you can do instead."

Lucy looked away, her voice barely a whisper. "I want to be a comedian, Sofia. But who's going to take me seriously? They'll just laugh because they think I'm a joke. My legs are paralyzed. I can't even walk around on the stage as I talk."

Sofia reached out and placed a hand on Lucy's. "Lucy, making people laugh is your superpower. You always say how happy it makes you when others are smiling. You have to share that with everyone! You won't know what people will think until you try."

Lucy sighed, still not convinced. "But what if they don't laugh? What if I mess up?"

Sofia grinned, squeezing her hand. "You're the funniest person I know, Lucy. You've got this!"

That evening, Sofia found herself sitting on her bed, her favorite book in hand, but she wasn't turning the pages. Her older sister Nina walked by the room and noticed Sofia's distant staring.

"What's wrong, Sofia? You're usually buried in that book. Something on your mind?"

Sofia looked up, her dark eyes troubled. "It's Lucy. She wants to be in the talent show, but she's scared. She thinks everyone will just see her wheelchair and not her talent. How can I help her?"

Nina sat beside Sofia, wrapping an arm around her shoulders. "You're already helping just by being there for her. But maybe you can give her a little push. Why not go with her to put her name on the sign-up sheet? And maybe offer to be help her with her act, or even offer to be a part of her act, so she won't be alone up there."

Sofia's eyes lit up as she nodded. "That's a great idea, Nina! Thanks!"

The next day, during their lunch break, Sofia and Lucy made their way to the talent show sign-up sheet. Sofia eagerly wrote her name down next to "Gymnastics Dance," and a smile spread across her face as she handed the pen to Lucy.

Lucy hesitated, staring at the pen like it was a venomous snake. "I can't do it, Sofia. I'm too scared."

Sofia turned to her with a determined look. "You have every right to participate, just like everyone else. And I'd love to help you with your act. You can do this. You're great." Lucy hesitated for a long time then suddenly grabbed the pen, reached forward, and wrote her name down on the sheet under "Comedy."

Just then, a group of students approached the sign-up sheet. Jillian, a girl with flowing auburn hair who was known for her love of poetry, wrote her name down for a poem recital. Manny, a tall boy with a confident stride, signed up for basketball dribbling, while Rohan, who always had a trick up his sleeve, listed his act as magic tricks.

As they finished signing up, Jillian turned to Lucy with a smirk. "What's your talent, Lucy? Wheelchair racing?"

Manny and Rohan snickered, and the trio walked away, leaving Lucy deflated. "See?" she whispered to Sofia. "They won't even see what I'm doing. They'll only see the wheelchair."

Sofia clenched her fists, anger bubbling up inside her at the bullies. "Come to my place after school," Sofia said firmly. "We're going to work on your act, and I know you'll blow everyone away."

Lucy reluctantly agreed. That afternoon, they found themselves in Sofia's living room, as Lucy nervously fiddled with her wheelchair's armrest.

"Okay, Luce, hit me with your best jokes," Sofia said, settling down on the floor, her hair fanning out around her.

Lucy hesitated and then began. Her voice was shaky at first but grew stronger as she continued. As Lucy delivered punchline after punchline, Sofia burst into laughter. The sound filled the room and lifted Lucy's spirits.

Nina, who had been listening from the doorway, joined them. "You've got great timing, Lucy. Just remember to make eye contact with your audience and keep them engaged."

The next day, Sofia and Lucy went to the school auditorium to practice. But there was a major problem—there was no ramp for Lucy to get onto the stage.

"This isn't fair," Sofia muttered, her frustration evident as she paced the empty auditorium. "You need to be able to get up there just like everyone else."

Determined, Sofia marched to Mrs. Ransen's classroom after school. "Mrs. Ransen, we need a ramp for the stage in the auditorium. Lucy can't perform if she can't get on the stage."

Mrs. Ransen smiled warmly at Sofia. "Thank you for bringing this to my attention, Sofia. I'll make sure a ramp is installed before the talent show."

True to her word, a few days later, a ramp was added to the stage. Sofia and Lucy tested it out, with Lucy rolling confidently onto the stage and her fears slowly melting away.

Even with the ramp, Lucy was still nervous. "Sofia, I'm not sure I can do this," Lucy admitted one afternoon. "I'm afraid of being up there all by myself."

Sofia put a reassuring hand on Lucy's shoulder. "Then let's make it a team act. If you use props, I'll come onstage with you and hand them to you during your act. That way, you won't be alone."

Lucy's eyes lit up with hope. "You'd do that for me?"

"Absolutely," Sofia replied without hesitation.

With renewed determination, they practiced together every day, fine-tuning Lucy's act. Sofia helped Lucy choose the right props, and by the end of the week, Lucy felt confident and excited for the big day.

Finally, the day of the talent show arrived. The auditorium buzzed with energy as students and teachers filled the seats, eager to see the performances.

Sofia's gymnastic dance for the talent show was an energetic performance that blended dance with powerful gymnastics. It went very well, and the audience seemed to like it. Sofia had been excited to perform her act, but was way more excited to help Lucy.

After her act, Sofia found Lucy backstage. Lucy was a bundle of nerves, her hands trembling as she adjusted her props.

Sofia knelt beside her, her voice gentle but firm. "Lucy, you've got this. Remember, making people laugh is your superpower. Just go out there and show them what you can do. I will be right beside you."

Lucy took a deep breath and nodded. "Okay. Let's do this."

When Lucy's turn came, Sofia rolled Lucy onto the stage, and the bright lights shone down on them. Sofia knew Lucy's heart was pounding in her chest as she faced the audience, but Sofia could tell it was helping that she was on the stage with her friend.

Taking a deep breath, Lucy launched into her act. She started with a joke about school lunches, then moved on to funny observations about their teachers. The audience began to chuckle, and as Lucy continued, their laughter grew louder. Throughout the act, Sofia handed Lucy her props and smiled at her friend encouragingly every chance she got.

The more the audience laughed, the more confident Lucy became. Her jokes flowed effortlessly, and soon the entire auditorium was filled with laughter. Sofia's heart swelled with pride as her best friend shone in the spotlight.

By the time Lucy delivered her final punchline, the audience was roaring with laughter and applause. Lucy beamed, her face glowing with happiness. She had done it—she had conquered her fears and won over the crowd.

After all the performances were finished, the judges announced the winners. Sofia's gymnastics dance took third and Rohan's magic show came in second. Lucy's comedic act took first place! The entire auditorium erupted in applause as Lucy wheeled forward to accept her trophy with a smile brighter than ever.

As students and teachers crowded around to congratulate Lucy, Sofia couldn't help but feel a sense of fulfillment. Jillian, Manny, and Rohan were among the first to approach Lucy. Their earlier teasing was forgotten as they praised her performance.

"You were amazing, Lucy," Jillian said sincerely, her eyes full of admiration. "I've never laughed so hard in my life."

"Yeah, you totally killed it," Rohan said with a grin. "I think we'll see your name in lights one day."

Lucy blushed and replied, "Thank you for your kind words. I was so nervous."

"Don't I know it," Rohan agreed. "I was sick in the boy's room just before I went on. I hope I can eliminate the stage fright if I do some shows in the future."

Lucy turned to Rohan. "Wait! You have stage fright?"

Rohan's eyes lifted. "For sure. It's awful."

"Me too," Jillian said, nodding in agreement. "It's nerve-wracking to be up there all alone. You're so lucky you had Sofia with you. That was super smart."

"It did make it easier," Lucy said.

"See, you're just like everyone else," Sofia reassured Lucy, happy that their classmates were sharing their feelings to make Lucy feel better.

As Sofia watched Lucy interact with Rohan, Jillian, and Manny, she couldn't help but be incredibly happy for her friend. She thought about how everyone deserves a chance to shine. Sofia was glad that Lucy had won first place and thought about how she had helped her win. It made her feel good inside that she could help Lucy realize her dreams, and she was happy that her best friend felt included and important.

"Why don't we celebrate at my house after school?" Sofia suggested. Lucy enthusiastically agreed.

On their way to Sofia's, Lucy said, "Thank you for all of your help, Sofia. I couldn't have done this without you."

"Of course you could have. You're much stronger than you think you are," Sofia encouraged her. "But next year, I'll try harder because I want first place."

"You'll have to beat me first," Lucy said with a grin.

"That sure will be tough, but I'm up for the challenge."

Lucy's smile didn't disappear for the rest of the evening, and neither did Sofia's.

Sofia helped her best friend Lucy overcome her fears and realize her talent for comedy, despite being nervous about performing in a wheelchair. The story shows that true friendship means supporting one another through challenges, and that everyone deserves a chance to shine. By believing in Lucy, Sofia proved that, with encouragement and determination, you can be brave even when you feel afraid.

The Science of Truth

Adaline Chevalier sat at her desk, her fingers nervously tapping on the edge of her notebook and twisting her long light-brown hair. Her gray eyes flickered with frustration. She had just turned 12 and was one of the brightest kids in her class, but when Mrs. Levine, her teacher, announced the upcoming science fair, and the entire class erupted in cheers, Adaline let out a low, frustrated moan.

"The science fair competition will take place in a month," Mrs. Levine continued, her voice full of excitement. "It's time to start thinking about your projects." Adaline slumped in her seat. The science fair was in a month?

Science was one of her favorite subjects, but science projects? They always filled her with dread. No matter how hard she tried, she could never think of a good idea, and, this year, she was determined to win. Last year, her rival, Andrew Roberts, had taken home first place with his elaborate volcano model, and Adaline was determined not to let him win again.

As the school day ended, and the students filed out of the classroom, Adaline's best friend Piper Dixxon caught up with her. Piper, with her wild, curly black hair and rebellious spirit, was the kind of person who never let anything get her down.

"What's up, Addie? You look like you just lost a million dollars," Piper said, her bright green eyes sparkling with curiosity.

Adaline sighed. "It's the science fair. I have no idea what to do. And Andrew—he's so smug about winning last year. I can't let him beat me again!"

Piper frowned. "Ugh, he thinks he's so smart. Whatever you do, don't let him win again. We've got to think of something."

The two girls spent the next few hours brainstorming ideas, but nothing seemed right. Piper suggested a crystal garden, but Adaline shook her head. "Andrew's going to come up with something even better. I need something unique, something that will blow everyone away."

When she arrived home, her mother, Collette, immediately noticed her mood. "What's wrong, my love?" she asked, her voice full of concern.

Adaline sighed and threw herself onto the couch. "It's the science fair, Mom. I can't think of what to do."

Her father, Pierre, who was in the kitchen preparing dinner, overheard the conversation and joined them. "Why not do a project with batteries? Or maybe something with magnets?" he suggested, always eager to help with ideas.

Adaline liked some of his suggestions, but she couldn't decide. "I don't know, Dad. I want to do something different, something amazing."

The next day at school, Piper was waiting for her at their usual spot by the lockers.

"Any luck with the science project?" Piper asked.

Adaline shook her head. "Not yet."

Piper frowned. "Just don't let Andrew win."

As the day dragged on, Adaline couldn't shake the feeling of impending failure. By the end of the day, she was no closer to a solution and was feeling more anxious than ever.

That evening, after a frustrating attempt to come up with a project on her own, Adaline was relieved when her mom knocked on her door.

"I've got an idea," Collette announced, holding up a notebook filled with sketches and notes. "How about a project on the different ways plants respond to light? You could use different colored lights to see how it affects their growth."

Adaline's eyes lit up. "That *does* sounds interesting. Thanks, Mom. Let me think about it for a bit."

Collette smiled, happy to help. "I thought it might help you learn more about something you already love."

Adaline thought about her mom's idea for the rest of the night. It made sense, since she loved plants and gardening so much. And it would help her learn more about her favorite hobby.

Adaline finally decided to go with her mom's idea and was determined to make it work. She spent the next few weeks working on her project in the living room and carefully setting up her experiment. Small pots with seedlings in them were lined up under makeshift light structures—one with a red bulb, another with a blue bulb, and a third with a regular white bulb. She diligently recorded the results as the plants slowly grew and changed. But no matter what she tried, the plants didn't seem to respond the way she had hoped. The leaves remained stubbornly the same, showing no significant difference in growth under the various lights.

"Ugh, this isn't working," she said out loud, frustrated. "They're supposed to show something by now!"

With the science fair deadline looming, panic set in. She fidgeted with her pencil and bit her lip as she looked at her plants, which all seemed to be about the same size. Her mind raced, thinking about her classmates and her teacher and how she desperately wanted to impress everyone with her project.

She stared at the chart, which was currently blank except for the headings "Red Light," "Blue Light," and "White Light." She picked up her pencil and tapped it against the paper as an idea formed in her mind.

"Well, it's just a little tweak. Everyone already knows red light is supposed to make plants grow taller, right?"

Desperate to win and terrified of failing, Adaline made a decision. She concocted fake results and altered her data to make it look as if her experiment had been a success. She scribbled down her "results" for the red light column, writing that those plants grew the strongest. For the blue light, she wrote that the plants grew slower but had thicker stems, and for the white light, she wrote that they grew at a normal pace.

She stepped back, looking at her work, then at the plants. Her heart beat a little faster. "It's just what everyone expects. It's not like they'll notice anyway." She wrote down her fake results on a posterboard and drew fake pictures of the plants. At first, she felt a sense of triumph, but it was quickly overshadowed by a gnawing guilt that she couldn't shake.

The night before the science fair, Adaline lay in bed and stared at the ceiling. The weight of her deception pressed down on her like a heavy blanket, making it impossible to sleep. She tried to convince herself that it didn't matter, that no one would find out, but, deep down, she knew she was lying to herself.

The day of the science fair arrived, and Adaline stood nervously by her project as her classmates and teachers walked around the room, examining the various experiments. Andrew was at the far end of the room, proudly showing off his project on electromagnetism.

When Mrs. Levine reached Adaline's station, she listened attentively as Adaline explained her project and pointed to the posterboard. But as she looked over the data, a frown creased her forehead.

"Adaline, this is very interesting," Mrs. Levine said, her voice kind but probing. "But some of these results seem unusual. Are you sure you followed the experiment correctly? And where are your plants?"

Adaline's heart raced, and her palms grew sweaty. She could feel the eyes of her classmates on her. She considered lying again, but the guilt was too much to bear. With her cheeks burning with shame, she finally spoke.

"No, Mrs. Levine. I—I faked the results. My experiment didn't work, and I didn't want to fail, so I made up the data."

A hush fell over the room as everyone stared at Adaline. She wanted to disappear, to melt into the floor and never have to face her peers again. But then Mrs. Levine did something unexpected. She placed a reassuring hand on Adaline's shoulder and smiled gently.

"Adaline, what you did was wrong, but it took a lot of courage to admit it in front of everyone. That's a lesson in integrity, and it's something to be proud of."

Adaline looked up, tears welling in her eyes, but Mrs. Levine's kind words gave her a sense of relief. Piper and a few other friends came up to her to offer words of comfort.

Another student, a girl named Marianne, stepped forward. "I also fudged my results a little," she confessed, her voice trembling. "It's really hard to get everything right."

Several other students nodded in agreement, sharing their own difficulties with their experiments. Mrs. Levine addressed the class with a warm smile. "Science is about exploration and learning, not just about getting the right answer. You shouldn't fake the results because it doesn't help anyone. If you're having trouble, you can always ask for help. That's what I'm here for."

Adaline felt a wave of relief wash over her. She had learned a valuable lesson, not just about science, but about honesty, integrity, and the importance of asking for help.

The classroom buzzed with anticipation as Mrs. Levine stepped up to the front of the room, holding the envelope that contained the name of the science fair winner. Adaline sat at her desk, her heart pounding in her chest.

Mrs. Levine smiled warmly at the class, her eyes scanning the eager faces before her. "I want to start by saying that each of you put in a lot of hard work, and I'm proud of all your efforts," she began. "But as you know, there can only be one winner."

Adaline swallowed hard, her gaze flickering to Andrew who sat a few rows ahead of her. She couldn't help but feel a twinge of envy, but she quickly pushed it aside. After all, she had learned the hard way that honesty was more important than winning. If she had only been honest about the results, even if they were unremarkable, perhaps she could have won.

Mrs. Levine slowly opened the envelope, the suspense in the room palpable. "And the winner of this year's science fair is Andrew Roberts, for his project on electromagnetism!"

The room erupted in applause, and, as she watched Andrew rise to accept his award, Adaline remembered the lesson she had learned. Andrew had worked hard on his project, and he deserved to be recognized for it.

As the applause died down, Mrs. Levine motioned for Andrew to say a few words. He stepped forward. "Thank you so much, Mrs. Levine. It was a tough competition, and I'm glad I could be a part of it."

Adaline made up her mind. She wasn't going to let her jealousy get the better of her. She walked over to where Andrew was packing up his project.

"Congratulations, Andrew" Adaline said, her voice steady and sincere.

Andrew looked up, a bit surprised by her approach. "Thanks, Adaline," he replied, his grin widening. But then he paused and said, "I wasn't sure I was going to make it this year. My experiment almost didn't work."

Adaline raised an eyebrow. "Really? But your project looked perfect."

Andrew shrugged, all traces of cockiness slipping away. "It wasn't at first. I had to redo the experiment a few times before it finally worked out. I was ready to give up more than once."

Adaline hesitated, then decided to take the plunge. "I've been having a lot of trouble with my experiment too. I guess that's why I did what I did."

Andrew nodded, his expression turning more thoughtful. "It happens. Science is tricky. Do you want to know why your experiment didn't work?"

Adaline blinked, taken aback by his offer. At first, her pride flared up—she wanted to refuse, to figure it out on her own. But then she remembered the lesson she had learned earlier that day. Asking for help wasn't a weakness- it was a strength.

"Yeah, I would," she said, smiling slightly. "If you have time, could you show me what I did wrong?"

Andrew's grin returned, this time without a hint of smugness. "Sure. I can come over to your house and look at the plants after school if that's okay."

Adeline nodded, feeling a sense of relief wash over her. "That would be great. Let me just ask my parents."

Later that afternoon, Andrew went to Adaline's house. They looked at her experiment still going on in the living room, and Andrew carefully examined the setup.

"Here's where you went wrong," he said after a moment. "Your light sources were too close to the plants. They need to be further away to simulate natural sunlight properly."

Adaline watched closely as Andrew adjusted the lights. She knew she wouldn't see the results right away, but she trusted him and would wait to see them later.

"That's incredible!" she exclaimed. "I didn't even think about that."

Andrew smiled, clearly pleased with her reaction. "It's all about trial and error. Sometimes it takes a few tries to get it right."

Adaline couldn't help but feel a newfound respect for Andrew. He wasn't just her rival—he was someone who understood the frustrations and joys of science as much as she did. "Thanks for helping me, Andrew. I really appreciate it."

"No problem," Andrew replied, his grin turning into a genuine smile. "We're all just trying to figure things out, right?"

As they packed up their notebooks, Adaline felt a sense of accomplishment that had nothing to do with winning. She learned that success achieved through deceit was hollow and that facing the consequences of her actions was the right thing to do. She had also made a new friend in the process.

Adaline realized something she hadn't expected: she was happy. Although she hadn't won the science fair, she had gained much more—a sense of integrity, a new friend, and a deeper understanding of what true success is. She had learned that success wasn't about beating someone else; it was about doing your best, learning from your mistakes honestly, and helping others along the way. And that, she realized with a smile, was the true victory.

> *Adaline learned that true success comes from honesty, perseverance, and helping others. When her science experiment didn't go as planned, she initially faked her results but later confessed. Because of her integrity, she gained a new friend and a deeper understanding of what it means to be truly successful. This story shows the importance of doing your best and learning from mistakes.*

Heritage and Heart

K ai Liu Zhang sat at her desk, absentmindedly curling her shoulder-
length black hair around her finger. Her black eyes were focused on
her best friend, Mei, who sat beside her, doodling in her notebook. The
classroom buzzed with excitement as their teacher, Ms. Perez, introduced
their next project.

"Class, we have two exciting activities coming up," Ms. Perez announced.
"First is an ancestry project in which you'll research your family background,
and second is a school-wide food drive to help local families in need."

Kai's heart sank a little. While she loved the idea of the food drive, the ancestry assignment made her feel anxious. At 11 years old, she felt disconnected from her Chinese heritage and was unsure where to start. Mei, sensing her friend's unease, nudged her gently.

"Kai, this could be fun! We can learn a lot about our families," Mei said with encouragement.

Kai managed a small smile. "Maybe, but I don't know much about my family's background. I'm feeling a bit nervous about it."

As the bell rang, signaling the end of the day, Ms. Perez called Kai over. "Kai, I know this project might seem challenging, but I believe you'll find it rewarding. Your family has a rich history worth exploring."

Kai nodded, appreciating her teacher's confidence. "Thank you, Ms. Perez. I'll do my best."

Walking home with Mei, Kai voiced her concerns. "Mei, how do you feel about the ancestry project?"

Mei grinned. "I'm excited! My grandparents love telling stories about their past. We can work on our assignments together. It'll be fun!"

Kai felt a bit more hopeful. "Thanks, Mei. Maybe I can ask my parents and grandparents for help too."

Kai's mind raced. The ancestry project seemed daunting enough, and now there was a food drive too. But maybe, she thought, they didn't have to be separate endeavors.

Kai sat in her room doing her homework when she got home from school. Sighing heavily, she looked at her dog, a miniature pinscher named Boots, who was resting on her bed, and asked, "Will you do my assignment for me?" Boots looked up at her, wagged his tail, then gave a "Ra-ruff!" as his answer. Kai giggled. "I'm hoping that's a *yes*." Worry formed in her stomach the more she thought about the assignment. How would she figure out a solution for both tasks when she had no clue what to do for either? Kai felt overwhelmed with self-doubt.

That evening, Kai decided to share her concerns with her family at the dinner table. Her parents, Yuyan and Jian Zhang, and her grandparents, Nai Nai and Ye Ye, were all present. Boots lay at her feet, looking up at her with curious eyes.

"Mama, Baba, I have an ancestry project to do for school, but I don't know where to start. And there's also a food drive. I'm not sure how to manage both."

Yuyan smiled gently. "We can help with your ancestry assignment, Kai. It's a wonderful opportunity to learn about our family's history."

Jian nodded. "As for the food drive, perhaps we can combine it with the other one. How about preparing traditional Chinese meals to share with the neighborhood?"

Kai's eyes lit up. "That sounds perfect! But I still need to learn more about our family's background."

Nai Nai, her grandmother, placed a hand on Kai's shoulder. "Let us tell you about our ancestors, Kai. You come from a long line of strong, resilient people. Our family history is rich with stories of courage and perseverance."

"Tell me, Nai Nai, where did our family come from?" Kai asked eagerly.

Nai Nai smiled warmly. "Our family comes from a small village in the Guangdong Province. Your great-great-grandparents were farmers, and they worked very hard to provide for the family. They grew rice and vegetables, and they also raised chickens."

Ye Ye chimed in, "Your great-grandfather moved to Hong Kong for better opportunities. He started a small business selling traditional Chinese medicines. That's where your grandfather and I lived before moving to America."

Kai scribbled down notes as they spoke, feeling a growing sense of connection to her family's history. "What about traditions? Are there any special customs or recipes passed down in our family?"

Nai Nai's eyes sparkled. "Oh, yes! We have many traditions, especially around food. During Lunar New Year, we make dumplings and sticky rice cakes. Your favorite, Kai, the red bean buns, were your great-grandmother's specialty."

Kai's eyes lit up. "I love red bean buns! Can you teach me how to make them?"

Yuyan smiled at her daughter's enthusiasm. "That's a wonderful idea, Mom. We can make some together and share them at the food drive."

Kai felt a growing sense of pride and connection to her family's past. She decided to incorporate these stories into her ancestry assignment She also thought about the food drive and how she could share her culture through traditional Chinese dishes.

The next few days were filled with bustling activity. Yuyan and Kai spent their evenings learning traditional recipes from Nai Nai. Boots watched curiously as Kai kneaded dough and mixed fillings, his tail wagging in anticipation of any scraps that might fall.

"Boots, no eating the dough!" Kai laughed, gently nudging her dog away from the counter. "Ra-ruff!" He then trotted around the kitchen, sniffing at the delicious aromas.

Yuyan guided Kai through each step, explaining the significance of the ingredients and the history behind the dishes. "These red bean buns symbolize prosperity and good fortune. Sharing them with others is a way to spread joy and blessings."

Kai nodded thoughtfully. "I want to share our traditions with everyone at the food drive. Maybe it will bring them some happiness too."

As they cooked, Kai also worked on her ancestry project. She created a family tree, complete with photos and stories shared by her grandparents. She felt a growing sense of pride and belonging with each new discovery.

The day of the food drive arrived, and Kai felt excited *and* nervous. The school gymnasium hummed with activity as students, parents, and teachers set up tables and organized donations. Kai and her mom carefully arranged their table with traditional Chinese dishes: red bean buns, dumplings, and sticky rice cakes. A sign read, "A Taste of Chinese Heritage."

Kai spotted her friend, Emma, across the room and waved. She'd always loved Emma's blond ringlets. Emma came over, her bright blue eyes widening at the sight of the food. "Wow, Kai! This looks amazing! Did you make all of this?"

Kai beamed with pride. "Yes, with help from my mom and grandparents. These are traditional Chinese dishes. Do you want to try some?" It shocked her that Emma was taking such an interest. Some of her other friends came over and tried the food too, and Kai felt incredible pride as she explained their origins.

Emma eagerly picked up a red bean bun and took a bite. "This is delicious! I had no idea your family had such cool traditions."

Kai felt a warm glow of pride. "Thanks, Emma. I'm learning a lot about my family's history, and it feels really good to share it with others."

As the food drive continued, more people stopped by Kai's table, curious about the dishes and their stories. She watched as people approached, curious about the unfamiliar foods. "Hello," Kai greeted them warmly. "Would you like to try some dumplings, red bean buns, and sticky rice cakes? These are traditional Chinese dishes, and my family and I made them together." Kai shared her family's history and traditions with everyone who asked, feeling more connected to her family's past with each conversation.

One woman smiled and took a dumpling. "These look wonderful. Thank you for sharing your culture with us."

Kai beamed. "You're welcome! I'm also working on an ancestry project for school, and I learned so much about my family's history. It's important to me to share that with others."

As the day passed, more people visited Kai's table, eager to try the food and learn about her heritage. Kai felt a deep sense of fulfillment. She was helping her neighborhood and sharing a part of herself.

It was time to present her ancestry project to the class the following week. Kai stood before the room, her family tree and photos displayed behind her.

"Hello, everyone. My name is Kai Liu Zhang, and I learned about my family's history and traditions for my ancestry assignment. My family comes from Guangdong Province in China, and we've kept many of our traditions alive through food. I also helped with the school food drive by sharing some traditional Chinese dishes, like red bean buns, dumplings, and sticky rice cakes. It was a way for us to give back and share our heritage with others. I've learned that discovering your roots gives you a sense of pride, and giving back to the community is a meaningful way to share your culture."

She glanced at her notes, feeling a surge of confidence. "This project taught me a lot about my heritage and made me feel closer to my family. When we share where we come from, we enrich our lives and the lives of those around us."

The class applauded, and Kai felt a deep sense of accomplishment. Ms. Perez smiled and said "Well done, Kai. Your project is an excellent example of how personal history and community service can go together."

After school, Kai walked home, feeling a new sense of connection to her heritage. She realized that celebrating her roots and helping others were powerful ways to enrich her life and the lives of those around her.

That evening, Kai and her family gathered for dinner. The table was filled with the delicious dishes they had made together. Boots sat at Kai's feet, hoping for a bite of his favorite red bean bun. "Everybody cheered after my presentation today," Kai said happily.

Nai Nai and Ye Ye approached, wrapping Kai in a warm embrace. "You did a wonderful job, Kai," Nai Nai said. "Your ancestors would be proud."

Kai smiled, feeling a warm sense of belonging. "Thank you, Nai Nai. I couldn't have done it without all of you. Thank you for helping me discover our history. I've learned that knowing where you come from and helping others are both important. It's like sharing a piece of ourselves with the world."

Yuyan nodded in agreement. "And it's a lesson that will stay with you forever, Kai."

Kai nodded, understanding the lesson deeply.

As they enjoyed their meal, Kai looked around at her family, feeling grateful for the journey they had taken together. She had discovered her heritage and found a way to give back, realizing that both were essential to her identity.

As the weeks passed, Kai volunteered at local events, sharing her family's traditions and stories. She also began to teach her classmates about Chinese culture and help them appreciate the beauty and richness of her heritage.

One day, while walking Boots in the park, Kai noticed a group of children playing together. She approached them with a smile.

"Hi, I'm Kai. Would you like to learn how to make paper lanterns? It's a tradition in my family."

The children eagerly agreed. She reached in her backpack and pulled out the supplies they needed. Soon, they were all sitting together, creating colorful lanterns and listening to Kai's stories about the Lantern Festival.

Right before the sun set, the lanterns almost looked liked they were glowing from the yellow light of the sky. Kai watched the children laugh and play and felt a deep sense of fulfillment. She had discovered her roots and found a way to share them with others, enriching her own life and the lives of those around her.

Kai knew that celebrating her heritage and helping her neighborhood were intertwined. By embracing both, she had found a way to honor her ancestors and make a positive impact on the world.

Looking down at Boots, who wagged his tail happily, Kai whispered, "We did it, Boots. We found a way to give back. And this is just the beginning."

With a heart full of pride and a spirit ready to serve, Kai Liu Zhang walked forward, ready to continue her journey of discovery and community service.

> *Kai learned that embracing her heritage and helping her community are powerful ways to enrich her life and the lives of those around her. By combining her ancestry assignment with the school food drive, she discovered the importance of sharing her culture and giving back. This experience taught her that celebrating her heritage and serving others go hand in hand.*

Stand Tall

Fiona Callahan stood at the corner of West 87th Street and Columbus Avenue, gripping her schoolbooks tightly to her chest. Her vibrant, curly red hair danced in the morning breeze, framing her freckled face. She was tall with green eyes. Fiona's heart raced as she looked down the street toward Riverside Elementary, the school she had attended since moving to Manhattan in September. It was now February, and her 10th birthday had come and gone, yet every day felt like a new battle.

"Ready, Fiona?" her best friend Heidi asked, adjusting her oversized glasses. Heidi was extremely short for her age; her glasses covered half her face.

"Aye, ready as I'll ever be," Fiona replied, her thick Irish accent evident. She tried to muster up a brave smile for her two best friends, but anxiety had clawed its way into her.

Sarah, who had thick brown hair down to her waist and was a bit overweight, gave Fiona a reassuring nod. "We'll stick together, right? Like always." Her voice trembled as if she didn't believe her own words.

"Aye, we will," Fiona affirmed, glancing at Heidi and Sarah.

As they walked through the school gates, Fiona could see Kyle, Derek, and Jack already waiting by the playground, smirking. Kyle, the ringleader, was tall and habitually flicked his hair back whenever he was about to say something mean.

"Look who it is," Kyle sneered as they approached. "The freckle-faced leprechaun and her sidekicks."

Fiona stepped forward, standing as tall as her 10-year-old frame allowed, and shakily said "Why are ye bothering us?" Her voice was quiet and she looked at the ground as she spoke.

Jack laughed, turning toward Fiona. "Maybe when you learn to speak like the rest of us, ye, we'll stop bothering you" Sometimes, Fiona felt like her thick Irish accent was a curse.

"Maybe we just don't like the way you look," Derek chimed in.

Heidi started to walk away and Kyle grabbed her glasses from her face, placed them on the ground, and kicked them with his foot. "Good luck finding those, four eyes."

Heidi shook her head and squinted. She looked like she was going to cry but held it in.

Fiona's stomach twisted but she said nothing.

"Give us your lunches NOW," said Derek. The girls looked at each other and then pulled out their sandwiches, handing them over. The boys snickered and walked away.

The next day, Fiona, Heidi, and Sarah met in the classroom to practice chess before class and started to strategize.

"We need to be smart about this," Fiona said, her green eyes shining with determination. "Let's pack foods they won't like. My mom can make a liver sandwich for me."

Heidi wrinkled her nose. "Gross, but a good idea. My mom can pack some weird-smelling cheese."

Sarah grinned. "And I'll bring some pickled herring. After that, they won't touch our lunches."

The classroom door banged open, and Kyle, Derek, and Jack walked in. Their eyes immediately locked onto the girls. Fiona felt a familiar knot of anxiety twist in her stomach. All she wanted to do was cry.

"Well, well, if it isn't Freckles, Shorty, and Fatso," Kyle sneered, leading the pack toward them.

Fiona stood up but was too scared to say anything. Her heart pounded.

"Whatcha gonna do?" Jack taunted, knocking the chess pieces off Fiona's desk. "Gonna cry to your mammy?"

Fiona clenched her fists, resisting the urge to fight them physically. Derek grabbed Sarah's lunch from her desk and tossing it to Kyle. "We like your lunches. Yum yum!"

Sarah's face fell, but she stayed silent, her eyes pleading with Fiona. Fiona knew she had to be the one to say something, anything.

"I'm telling Principal Farragher," Fiona whispered unconvincingly.

"Tell him all you want," Kyle laughed. "He won't do anything."

The bell rang, and their teacher entered the room. The boys slunk back to their seats, snickering. Fiona sat down, her heart heavy. She had hoped that at some point the bullies would simply go away, but it seemed like nothing would change.

The next day at lunch, Fiona, Heidi, and Sarah were hoping to eat peacefully. Peace was rare these days.

"Heidi, how are yer glasses holdin' up?" Fiona asked, noticing the crack in one of the lenses getting bigger.

Heidi's hand flew up to adjust them. "My parents are getting tired of replacing them."

"Maybe we should actually talk to Principal Farragher," Sarah suggested, picking at her food. "He's the only one who may understand."

Fiona nodded. "Aye, we should do that sometime."

They fell quiet, eating their lunches.

"Hey, freaks," Kyle's voice cut through the silence.

"Why are you here?" Fiona said quietly, her voice a scared whisper.

"Because it's fun," Derek said, snatching Sarah's sandwich and taking a big bite. "Ew, what is this? It tastes awful."

Fiona's eyes twinkled with a hint of triumph. "My mom packed us food ye don't like. Guess ye'll have to find someone else to steal from."

Kyle's face twisted in annoyance. "We'll see about that."

The next day, the boys didn't steal any lunches, but they found other ways to make the girls' lives miserable. During recess, Derek tripped Heidi, completely breaking her glasses. Sarah started crying as and Fiona held back tears.

"Enough!" Principal Farragher's voice boomed from behind them. He had seen the whole thing. "Kyle, Derek, Jack- my office, now!"

As the boys sulked off, Principal Farragher turned to the girls. "Are you three alright?"

Heidi nodded, though tears streamed down her face. "My glasses..."

"We'll get them fixed," Mr. Farragher assured her. "But we need to talk. Come to my office after lunch."

Later, the girls sat in Mr. Farragher's office, the atmosphere tense but hopeful.

"Girls, I know it's tough, but you have to come to me when these events occur. How long has this been going on?"

The girls took some time to explain all the bullying from the three boys and how long it had gone on.

"I'm sorry this has been happening," Mr. Farragher said, his tone gentle. "I had a firm chat with those boys, and I have suspended them for three days. I will also talk to their parents. If this happens again, please come to me."

"We should have come to ye sooner," Fiona said quietly. "They keep bothering us. I want to punch them every time."

"They're nonstop," Sarah said softly. "What if it *never* stops?"

"It will," Principal Farragher said. "Keep seeking help from me and other teachers, and we will keep punishing them. Meanwhile, when they're back from suspension, if they bother you again you just need to use your words calmly with them, tell them to stop, and, if you can, walk away. It's not worth fighting them- two wrongs don't make a right. Then come to me and let me know."

Fiona nodded, absorbing his words. "What if they corner us again?"

"Standing up to bullies isn't always easy or immediate," he began. "Report every incident to me, another teacher or a parent. We're here to help you. Always stick together and try not to have lunch alone."

"Thanks, Principal Farragher," Heidi said, her voice wavering but grateful.

"One more thing," Principal Farragher added. "Change your routines. Eat lunch in different places and take different routes to class. Don't let them figure out your patterns."

The next few weeks were challenging, but Fiona, Heidi, and Sarah followed Mr. Farragher's advice. They varied their routines and stayed together.

One afternoon, as the girls were heading home, the bullies cornered them. Jack sneered at Fiona. "Nice hair, Carrot Top. And those freckles—did someone splatter paint on you?"

Fiona was ready for this moment. She stood tall and said "Leave us alone, Jack. Your words can't hurt us."

Kyle tried to trip Heidi. "Oops. Too short to see where you're going, Heidi?"

Heidi burst into tears, and Sarah tried to shield her. "Stop it! Why are you so mean?"

"Because it's fun," Derek said with a smirk.

Fiona's fists clenched, but she remembered Mr. Farragher's advice that two wrongs don't make a right. "We're not going to fight you. We just want to be left alone."

"Yeah, right," Jack scoffed. "Like we'll listen to you."

The girls walked away. They felt defeated but refused to give up.

The next day, they talked to Principal Farragher again.

"They won't stop," Fiona explained, her voice filled with frustration.

Principal Farragher frowned. "I'm sorry to hear that. I will do what I can on my end. We'll get this resolved together. I will get them suspended again."

Although the boys were suspended for another 3 days, once they returned, they were back to their old habits, cornering the girls once more as they headed to the library. This time, Fiona stood in front of her friends, her eyes blazing with determination.

"Give it a rest, Kyle," she said, her voice steady. "We're not afraid of ye anymore."

Kyle sneered but hesitated. Fiona's calm confidence seemed to unnerve him. Derek and Jack exchanged uncertain glances.

"You think you're so tough," Kyle muttered, but his words had less conviction.

"We are tough," Fiona replied. "We're not going to let ye get to us anymore."

"You think you can hide from us?" Kyle sneered. "Think again."

"We're not hidin'," Fiona said, her voice steady. "We're standin' up for ourselves."

Jack lunged forward, but Fiona stood her ground. "Stop," she said firmly. "We're not afraid of ye."

The boys hesitated, taken aback by her confidence. Derek scoffed. "Whatever. You're all freaks anyway."

Fiona felt a surge of anger but remembered Principal Farragher's words. "We're not freaks. We're friends. And we're not gonna let ye bully us anymore."

Kyle glared at them, but his eyes flickered with uncertainty. "Come on, guys," he muttered. Let's go."

The boys glared at them but eventually walked away, muttering under their breaths. As the boys left, Fiona let out a breath she hadn't realized she was holding. Heidi and Sarah hugged her tightly.

"You were amazing, Fiona," Heidi said, her voice full of admiration.

"We did it together," Fiona replied, smiling at her friends. "And we'll keep doin' it until they leave us alone."

"Do you think it's over?" Sarah asked, her voice hopeful.

Fiona shrugged. "Maybe not, but we'll keep standing up to them. Together."

Days turned into weeks, and the boys' bullying began to wane. The boys still made the occasional snide comments, but the intensity had lessened. The boys laughed when the girls walked by, but didn't come near them anymore. Fiona, Heidi, and Sarah grew more confident, their bond stronger than ever.

One sunny afternoon, as the girls sat peacefully by the playground, Fiona looked at her friends with a smile. "We did it, didn't we?"

Heidi adjusted her new glasses and nodded. "Yeah, but they still make fun of us," she reminded them.

Sarah grinned. "True, but they're leaving us alone. Besides, we're sticking together, so we'll just keep fighting them if they try again. Eventually, they'll get bored."

Fiona's heart swelled with pride. She had learned an important lesson: Standing up for yourself was crucial, even if it didn't bring immediate results. Plus, talking to a trusted adult had helped. Persistence, support, and courage made all the difference.

As they walked home that day, Fiona felt a sense of peace. Manhattan had become a little brighter and a little safer, all because three friends refused to back down, plus asked for help.

"Ready for a game of chess later?" Fiona asked, her eyes sparkling.

Heidi and Sarah laughed. "You bet!"

Fiona knew she had the strength and the friends to face whatever came next. Together, they could handle anything.

Fiona learned that standing up to bullies takes persistence, courage, and the support of true friends and trusted adults. Even when it seemed like nothing would change, Fiona and her friends stuck together, refused to back down, and found strength in their unity. Fiona discovered that facing challenges with determination and the right people by your side can make all the difference.

Facing the Fear

L eisel Zimmerman felt like her world was crashing down around her. At 12 years old, she had always been the quiet, sweet girl who preferred to stay in the background rather than draw attention to herself. She spent most of her days reading books about faraway lands and magical creatures, where the characters never had to deal with the awkwardness of growing up. But lately, her own body seemed determined to make her the center of attention, whether she wanted it to or not. She was short with blond ringlets and hazel eyes and was self-conscious of the fact that she wasn't as thin as all her friends.

Leisel stood in front of her bedroom mirror, frowning at her reflection. Her once-flat chest had started to fill out, and her mother had recently taken her shopping for bras—an experience Leisel would rather forget. The sensation of wearing a bra felt strange, and she couldn't shake the feeling that everyone at school would notice. Worse still, her hips had begun to widen, and the curves that her mother called "beautiful" only made Leisel want to hide. Liesel's mother told her that her beautiful curvy body was because of her German heritage, along with her blue eyes and dirty blond hair.

As Liesel dressed for gym class that day, she pulled on her gym clothes with a heavy heart. What used to be her favorite part of the school day had become a daily source of anxiety. The thought of running around in front of her classmates, her body jiggling in ways it never had before, was mortifying. She tried her best to stay out of sight, often pretending to tie her shoelaces just as the teacher called for volunteers to demonstrate exercises.

Today, however, Liesel's worst fears came true. She started her period right before gym class. It was the third month ever of Liesel getting her period, and her mother had already shown her how to attach a pad to her underwear. But during gym glass, the pad always seemed to move around. Liesel was so worried that the pad would accidentally fall out of her shorts, which caused her a ton of anxiety.

During class, the teacher had the class run laps around the track. Leisel kept her pace slow, hoping to blend in with the others. But then, as she rounded the corner on her third lap, she felt something shift. A cold dread settled in her stomach. Her pad had slipped. She could feel it moving, no longer in the place it was supposed to be, and she panicked.

Leisel tried to adjust it a few times as she slowed to a walk, but it was too late. A few girls nearby had noticed her odd behavior and started whispering to each other. Leisel's face burned with embarrassment. She could hear their giggles, and it felt like the sound was echoing off the walls, amplifying her shame. She wanted to disappear.

"Hey, Leisel, you okay?" one of the girls, Madison, called out with a smirk. She was standing with the popular girls; the others were Kelly, Nancy, and Andrea.

"What's the matter? You got ants in your pants?" Andrea yelled out.

"More like her big boobs hit her in the eye," Nancy called out, which brought on a fit of laughter from the four girls.

Leisel didn't answer. She kept her head down, praying for the class to end. Her heart pounded in her chest, and her eyes welled with tears. All she could think about was getting out of there. She had never felt so humiliated in her life.

When the teacher finally blew the whistle, signaling the end of class, Leisel bolted to the locker room. She could still hear the whispers and snickers behind her, each one like a dagger to her already fragile self-esteem. She quickly changed out of her gym clothes and stuffed her pad deep into the trash can, hoping no one would notice. She then put a new one on and made sure it was secure.

Leisel spent the rest of the day in a daze. She couldn't focus on her schoolwork, and the idea of facing her classmates again the next day made her stomach churn. By the time she got home, she had made up her mind: she was never going back to gym class. She would fake an illness or maybe even skip school entirely—anything to avoid the humiliation she had endured.

That evening, Leisel sat at the dinner table, pushing her food around her plate. Her mother, Annika, noticed her daughter's uncharacteristic silence.

"Leisel, sweetie, are you feeling okay?" her mother asked gently.

Leisel looked up, her eyes full of unshed tears. She had always been close to her mother, confiding in her about everything from her favorite books to her fears about growing up. But this was different. This was something she wasn't sure she could talk about, but she felt so alone and needed to talk to someone.

"Mom," Leisel began, her voice trembling, "something really embarrassing happened today at school."

Annika reached across the table and took Leisel's hand in hers. "Oh, honey, I'm sorry. Do you want to talk about it?"

Leisel hesitated, but the warmth in her mother's eyes gave her the courage she needed. She recounted the events of gym class, her voice barely above a whisper, and when she finished, she felt the tears spill over and run down her cheeks.

"I just don't want to go back to school, Mom," Leisel confessed, wiping her eyes. "Everyone was laughing at me. I don't know how I can face them again."

Annika's heart ached for her daughter. She had gone through her own awkward stages growing up and knew how painful it could be. She pulled Leisel into a comforting embrace.

"Leisel, I know it feels like the end of the world right now, but I promise you, it's not," Annika said softly. "These things happen to everyone, especially when you're going through changes like you are."

Leisel looked up at her mother, her eyes searching for reassurance. "Did—did anything like this ever happen to you?"

Annika smiled, a nostalgic look crossing her face. "Oh, absolutely. I remember one time in middle school, I had just gotten my period, and I was so nervous about it. I thought I had everything under control, but during math class, I realized I had leaked through my white pants. I was mortified, Leisel. I thought I would die of embarrassment."

Leisel's eyes widened. "What did you do?"

"Well," Annika continued, "I wrapped my sweater around my waist and tried to hide it the best I could. But then, a classmate noticed and pointed it out. I wanted to crawl under my desk and never come out."

Leisel's mouth dropped open. "That's awful, Mom! What happened after that?"

"I ran to the bathroom and cried," Annika admitted. "But when I got home, I talked to my mom about it, and she told me something that really helped. She said that growing up can be messy and awkward, and everyone goes through embarrassing moments like that. It doesn't define you. What defines you is how you handle it afterward."

Leisel listened intently, absorbing every word. "So, what should I do, Mom?"

Annika took a deep breath and chose her words carefully. "First of all, I think you need to give yourself some grace- periods are healthy, normal, and natural. What happened today was unfortunate, but it doesn't mean everyone will remember it forever. Kids can be mean sometimes, but most of the time, they're just trying to deal with their own insecurities. Tomorrow, if you act like it's no big deal, chances are they'll forget about it soon enough."

Leisel nodded slowly, still unsure but willing to trust her mother. "But what about gym class? I don't know if I can go back."

"I understand that, sweetheart," Annika said, stroking Leisel's hair. "But you shouldn't let one bad experience keep you from doing the things you enjoy. Here's what we can do. I'll show you some ways to make sure your pad stays in place during gym class. We can even try using different kinds of products and different pad sizes until you find what works best for you."

Leisel bit her lip. "Do you really think that'll help?"

"I do," Annika said confidently. "And if you ever feel unsure, you can always come to me. We'll figure it out together. You're not alone in this, Leisel."

The warmth and love in her mother's voice made Leisel feel a little better. She knew her mom was right— running away from her problems wasn't the answer. Maybe, just maybe, she could face her fears and get through this.

The next morning Leisel woke up and her stomach immediately twisted with anxiety. She had spent the evening talking with her mother, learned how to use a tampon, trying out different size pads, and practicing how to discreetly adjust her pad if needed. Her mom even shared a few more stories from her own teenage years, which made Leisel feel a little less alone in her struggles.

As Leisel walked into the school building, she felt a flutter of nerves in her stomach. But she reminded herself of her mother's words: Everyone goes through embarrassing moments. It doesn't define you.

When it was time for gym class, Leisel took a deep breath and joined her classmates. She noticed Madison and the other girls from the previous day whispering to each other again, and for a moment, her confidence wavered. But then she squared her shoulders, deciding she wouldn't let them get to her.

As they started their warm-up exercises, Leisel kept an eye on herself, making sure everything was in place. She followed the tips her mother had given her, and, to her relief, everything seemed fine. The whispers continued, but Leisel ignored them and focused on her own movements.

When they began to run laps, Leisel felt a twinge of fear. What if it happened again? But she pushed the thought aside and kept going. With each step, her confidence grew. She could do this. She was prepared.

After gym class ended, Leisel went to the locker room with a sense of relief. She had made it through without any disasters. As she changed back into her regular clothes, she overheard Madison talking to another girl.

"Did you see Leisel today? She seemed totally fine," Madison said, almost sounding disappointed.

"Yeah, I thought she'd freak out again, but she didn't," the other girl replied.

Leisel smiled to herself. They had expected her to crumble, but she hadn't. She had faced her fears and come out stronger on the other side. Maybe gym class wasn't so scary after all.

When Leisel got home that afternoon, her mother waited for her in the kitchen. "How was your day, sweetie?" Annika asked, handing Leisel a glass of lemonade.

Leisel grinned. "It was great! I did everything you said, and the other girls were still talking about me behind my back, but I didn't let that bother me, and then they stopped. Mom, they stopped!"

"That's terrific, Leisel," Annika exclaimed. "Seeking advice and support from trusted adults, such as me," her mother smiled and winked, "can really help you find solutions and support through tough times. I'm so proud of you honey."

As her mother hugged her, Leisel thought about how she had dealt with the situation and felt confident that she could handle almost anything as long as she faced her fears and kept trying. Leisel also realized how relieved she was that she'd opened up to her mom, who really helped her. She couldn't stop grinning for the rest of the night.

> *Leisel learned that growing up comes with challenges and awkward moments, but facing them with courage and support makes all the difference. By listening to her mother's advice and staying strong, she discovered that she could handle anything, even the toughest situations. For any girl reading, remember: You're stronger than you think, and seeking help when needed is a sign of true strength.*

The Power of Pause

Sidney Rosewell stared at her meticulously organized calendar with a frown. Every square inch of it was filled with activities, clubs, practices, and study sessions. There was no time for anything unplanned. Her marks at school were in the high 90s, and she was determined to become a brain surgeon someday. But lately, something felt off. Sidney wasn't sure what the issue was, but a sense of unease had settled in her chest.

At lunchtime, Sidney went into the bathroom and studied her reflection in the mirror, trying to find out what was wrong with her. Tired light green eyes stared back at her. She looked at her long, straight blond hair and wondered if she should get her hair cut really short. It would take less time to maintain if it were above her ears and free her up to do more things. She smiled and returned to join her best friend Robin Hart in line at the school cafeteria.

Robin sat across from her several minutes later, munching on a sandwich. "You look stressed, Sidney," Robin observed, her eyes full of concern.

"I'm fine," Sidney replied, her voice tight. "I just have so much to do. Science club, math club, chess club, Girl Scouts... not to mention baseball and lifeguard practice. And I have to keep up with my reading too."

Robin raised an eyebrow. "You're always busy. Do you ever just, you know, take a break?"

Sidney sighed, rubbing her temples. "There's no time for breaks, Robin. If I take a break, I'll fall behind. Everyone's counting on me."

Robin reached across the table and gently placed her hand over Sidney's. "Maybe you should pick your favorite activities and let the others go. It's okay to slow down, you know."

Sidney shook her head vehemently. "No, I can't do that. Everyone needs me. And besides, what if I miss something important?"

Robin sighed, knowing it was pointless to argue with Sidney when she was in this mood. "Just don't forget to take care of yourself, okay? You're not a machine."

Sidney nodded absentmindedly, her mind already drifting to her next task. But Robin's words lingered, and a small seed of doubt grew in the back of her mind.

Later that evening, Sidney was in her room, surrounded by textbooks and notes. She was in the middle of solving a complex math problem when her mother's voice called up the stairs.

"Sidney! Dinner's ready!"

Sidney frowned at the interruption. She was in the zone, and the last thing she wanted was to stop for dinner. "I'll take my plate up here!" she called back, already grabbing her pencil to continue her work.

A few moments later, her mother, Lila, appeared in the doorway with a stern expression. "No, Sidney. We're all eating together tonight."

Sidney looked up in surprise. "But Mom, I have so much to do—"

"And it can wait," Lila said firmly. "Your father and I have decided that we're starting a new tradition. We're going to have dinner together as a family once a week, and I expect you to be there."

Sidney's heart sank. This was going to mess up her entire schedule. "But Mom, I can't! I have so much on my plate already—"

Lila held up a hand to stop her. "I know you're busy, Sidney. But family is important, and you have to make time for us too. So, please, come downstairs."

Sidney reluctantly followed her mother to the dining room, where her father, Carmen, and her younger brother, Evan, were already seated. Her older sister, Carly, was putting down her phone as Sidney sat down. Sidney's face clearly showed she would rather be elsewhere.

The dinner started off quietly, with Sidney eating as fast as she could. Her mind raced with everything she still needed to do, and she barely heard the conversation around her.

"Sidney, slow down," her father said gently. "You don't need to rush."

"But I have so much to do," Sidney mumbled through a mouthful of food.

"Well, you're not leaving this table until everyone's finished eating," Carmen said with a finality that made Sidney's stomach twist.

Sidney groaned inwardly. This was going to be torture. She watched in dismay as everyone ate at a leisurely pace, seemingly oblivious to the time ticking away.

Finally, Sidney couldn't take it anymore. "Why are you all eating so slowly?" she blurted out, her frustration spilling over.

Her mom gave her a patient smile. "We're enjoying our meal, Sidney. And we'd like you to enjoy it with us."

Sidney bit back a retort and forced herself to sit quietly until everyone was finished. As soon as they were done, she bolted from the table and rushed back to her room, her heart pounding. This new dinner tradition was going to ruin everything!

The next day, Sidney vented her frustrations to Robin during their lunch break. "I can't believe my parents are making me do this! It's such a waste of time."

Robin listened patiently, nodding along. "I get it, Sidney. But maybe it's not such a bad thing. I mean, I eat with my parents every night from Sunday to Thursday. It's nice to catch up with them."

Sidney looked at Robin skeptically. "I had no idea you ate with them almost every night. You like it?"

Robin shrugged. "Yeah, it's nice. We talk about our day and stuff like that. It's a great way to stay connected."

Sidney thought about Robin's words a week later as she sat at the dinner table with her family again. She decided to give Robin's advice a try so she asked her dad about his day at work.

Her dad's eyes lit up as he started to talk about a new project he was working on. Sidney listened, genuinely interested, and found herself asking more questions. Carly chimed in with a funny story about something that happened at school, and even Evan shared a bit about his hockey practice.

To Sidney's surprise, the dinner was actually enjoyable. She found herself laughing at Carly's jokes and getting excited about her father's project. For the first time in a long time, Sidney felt a sense of connection with her family.

As the weeks passed, Sidney began to look forward to the family dinners. She learned so much about her parents and siblings- things she never would have known if she had stayed holed up in her room. She discovered that her mother had a passion for gardening and that her father was an excellent cook. It turned out that Carly was not simply obsessed with makeup and boys— she was actually funny and had a sharp wit that Sidney hadn't noticed before. Even Evan surprised her with his sports knowledge and dedication to his hockey team.

Slowly, Sidney began to reevaluate her priorities. She realized that while she loved all of her activities, she didn't need to do them all. She dropped a few that she didn't enjoy as much and found that she had more time to spend with her family.

She started going on nature walks with Carly, who turned out to be a great hiking companion. They would talk about everything and nothing, and Sidney found herself opening up in ways she never had before. She also started tossing a baseball around with Evan in the backyard, which became a fun way to unwind after a long day.

Sidney even took an interest in her father's work and her mother's gardening. She helped cook with her father and found that cooking was quite relaxing,. When she gardened with her mother, she found that gardening was a peaceful escape from the chaos of her busy life.

One evening, as they all sat down for dinner, Sidney looked around the table at her family and felt content. She realized how much she had come to value these moments with them.

"I'm grateful for these dinners," Sidney said suddenly, surprising herself and everyone else.

Her dad smiled at her, pride in his eyes. "We're grateful to have you here with us, Sidney."

Her mom reached across the table and squeezed Sidney's hand. "It means a lot to us that you've been making time for our family."

Sidney nodded, a lump forming in her throat. She hadn't realized how much she had missed out on by always being so focused on her activities. Now, she couldn't imagine life without these dinners.

Months passed, and Sidney continued to make time for her family. She excelled in school and still aimed to become a brain surgeon one day, but she was no longer driven solely by the need to achieve. She had learned to appreciate the simple, everyday moments that brought her closer to the people she loved.

One evening, after dinner, Sidney sat out on the porch with her father and watched the sunset.

"You've grown up a lot, Sidney," Carmen said. "I'm really proud of you."

Sidney smiled up at him. "Thanks, Dad. I've learned a lot this year."

He put his arm around her shoulders, and they sat in comfortable silence, watching as the sky turned shades of pink and orange.

Sidney had always been smart and driven. But now she understood that true wisdom wasn't just about knowing things—it was about understanding the value of family, the importance of gratitude, and the beauty of the world around her.

As she looked out at the horizon, Sidney felt a deep sense of peace. She still had big dreams and wanted to achieve great things, but now she knew that the journey was just as important as the destination. She was grateful to have her family by her side every step of the way.

Sidney's story teaches us that, while pursuing dreams and keeping up with your work is important, it's equally crucial to make time for family and self-care. By slowing down and connecting with her loved ones, Sidney discovered that balance brings true fulfillment. Prioritizing relationships and appreciating simple moments can enrich your life and make the journey toward your goals even more meaningful.

Changing Her Tune

Polly McFadden was not one to blend in, even if she tried. With her bright, thick red hair that practically glowed in the sunlight, green eyes that sparkled with curiosity, and a face full of freckles, she was a sight to behold. Standing tall for her age, she was also lanky and had the kind of uncoordinated movements that made her seem perpetually on the brink of a tumble. Burlington, Vermont, was a far cry from the small Scottish village she had called home just a few months before, and now, at 12 years old, Polly was trying to fit into the complex world of middle school in a brand-new city.

"Ye'll do just fine," her mother had reassured her that morning as Polly stood nervously by the front door, her backpack hanging loosely over one shoulder. "Jest be yerself, lass."

But being herself wasn't as simple as it sounded, especially when "being herself" meant tripping over her own feet in front of her classmates or accidentally spilling her lunch tray in the cafeteria. Polly had learned quickly that middle school wasn't a place where clumsiness was easily forgiven. So she kept to herself, hoping to go unnoticed.

That was until she met Tamara.

Tamara was a whirlwind of energy and confidence, the kind of girl who could light up a room just by walking into it. She had short, curly hair, dark brown skin, and an infectious smile that seemed to melt away any of Polly's shyness.

"Hi! You're new here, right?" Tamara had asked on Polly's second day, practically bouncing over to her during recess.

Polly nodded, not trusting herself to say much.

"Cool! I'm Tamara. You should totally join some after-school activities with me. It's a great way to meet people and, you know, find your thing!"

Polly blinked at her. "M-me?"

"Yes, you! C'mon, it'll be fun. There's jazz, tap, ballet, gymnastics, clubs... You name it, we've got it! You just have to try things out and see what fits."

Polly wasn't sure anything would fit, but Tamara's enthusiasm was hard to resist. Before she knew it, Polly found herself signing up for more activities than she'd ever dreamed of.

First up was dance. Polly wasn't entirely convinced this was a good idea, given her tendency to trip over her own two feet, but she figured it was worth a shot. Maybe, just maybe, she'd find some hidden grace within herself.

The reality of jazz class hit her like a ton of bricks. Within the first 10 minutes, Polly had managed to collide with three other students, tangle herself in the ribbons of her jazz shoes, and somehow end up flat on her back, staring at the ceiling.

"Are you okay?" Macy, a girl with short blonde hair and big blue eyes, asked, offering her a hand to pull herself up up.

Polly accepted the hand, her cheeks flushing with embarrassment. "Aye, just need tae work on me landin', I suppose."

Macy laughed, and Polly found herself smiling despite her bruised ego. Maybe she wasn't cut out for jazz, but at least she had made a new friend.

Next, Polly tried tap, which was even worse. The rhythm was impossible to follow, and every time she tapped her toes, she ended up kicking the person in front of her.

"Sorry! Sorry!" Polly muttered repeatedly, her face burning even redder than usual.

Ballet was no better. Her lanky limbs refused to move in sync with the graceful girls around her, and the instructor's constant corrections only made her more self-conscious. Polly couldn't help but feel like a giraffe in a room full of swans.

Gymnastics, she quickly discovered, was a no-go as well. Polly had barely managed a forward roll when she smacked her elbow on the mat and winced in pain.

"Maybe this isn't for me," Polly said to herself as she nursed her bruised arm.

But she kept going. If there was one thing Polly was good at, it was perseverance. She joined the chess club, only to find the strategies baffling. The science club was fun, especially when it came to the experiments, but she felt out of her depth when discussions got too technical. The computer club was boring, though she did meet a boy named Greg who was kind and always treated her nicely.

One afternoon, while sitting alone at lunch, Polly saw Tamara approaching with a tray full of food and an even bigger smile.

"How's it going, Polly? Found your thing yet?"

Polly sighed. "Not yet, Tamara. It seems like I'm hopeless at everything."

Tamara shook her head vigorously. "No way! You're just exploring. You'll find something that makes you happy. I'm sure of it."

Polly wanted to believe her, but her confidence was wearing thin. That afternoon, she walked into the newspaper club, thinking it might be her last attempt before giving up entirely. The club advisor, Mrs. Peters, assigned her to the poetry column, and Polly hesitated. She had never thought of herself as a writer, let alone a poet.

"Give it a try," Mrs. Peters encouraged. "You might surprise yourself."

To Polly's shock, she did. Words flowed out of her like they'd been waiting for the right moment. She crafted a poem about a redheaded girl lost in a forest, searching for a place to belong. Mrs. Peters praised her work, and for the first time since moving to Burlington, Polly felt a glimmer of pride.

Her real moment of discovery came by accident, as so many things in Polly's life did. One day, as she was leaving school, she heard the most beautiful music floating through the hallway. The sound was warm and rich and seemed to vibrate in the air around her. Polly followed the music to the source, finding herself at the door of the music room.

Peeking inside, she saw students playing various instruments, but her eyes were drawn to one in particular—a cello. The student playing it was swaying gently with the music, and the deep, resonant notes made Polly's heart ache in the best way possible.

She stood there for several minutes, entranced, until the music stopped, and the students began to pack up.

"Hey, are you interested in joining the music club?" a voice asked from behind her. Polly jumped, turning to find a tall girl with fiery red hair much like her own. "I'm Lucy. I play the harp."

Polly nodded, her voice catching in her throat. "Aye, I think I'd like that if it's not too late."

Lucy grinned. "It's never too late! What instrument are you thinking about?"

Polly's gaze drifted back to the cello. "That one. It's... beautiful."

"Good choice!" Lucy said, her eyes lighting up. "Why don't you talk to Mr. Ellis, the music teacher? I'm sure he'd love to have you in the club."

That night, Polly could barely contain her excitement. As soon as she got home, she rushed into the kitchen where her mother was preparing dinner.

"Mum, can I join the music club? I want to learn the cello!"

Her mother paused, setting down the knife she was using to chop vegetables. "The cello? That's a lovely instrument, Polly. Aye, and it reminds me of yer grandpa. Did ye know he used to play in an orchestra?" Her mother smiled warmly, a hint of sadness in her eyes. "Aye, he did. He'd be so proud tae see ye followin' in his footsteps."

Polly's heart swelled. "So can I join?"

"Of course ye can, lass. Ye'll need tae practice a lot, though."

"That's fine! I'll practice every day!"

Polly's little brother Finn snorted from the living room. "Good luck with that, Polly. Ye're clumsy enough as it is. Ye'll probably end up breakin' it!"

Polly stuck her tongue out at him but ignored his teasing, too excited to let it bother her. After dinner, her mother sat down with her, and they talked about her new musical venture. Polly felt a connection to her grandfather she hadn't felt since he passed away two years earlier.

The next day, Polly approached Mr. Ellis after school. He was a kind, middle-aged man with graying hair and glasses that constantly slipped down his nose.

"I'd like tae join the music club and learn the cello," Polly said, trying to keep her nerves in check.

Mr. Ellis smiled. "We'd be happy to have you, Polly. The cello is a wonderful instrument. Do you have one, or will you need to borrow one from the school?"

Polly hesitated. "I dinnae have one yet."

"No problem. We have a spare. Let's get you started."

And so, Polly began her lessons. The cello was harder to play than she had imagined, and, at first, the notes she produced were more screeches than music. But she was determined, and, with each practice session, she improved a little more.

One afternoon, as she went to her room to practice the borrowed cello from the music room, she noticed another cello in the corner of the room with a bow on top of it and a small note from her parents:

"We found Grandpa's cello. It's yours now. Practice times are on the schedule below so ye dinnae drive us crazy. Love, Mum and Dad."

Polly's eyes filled with tears as she gently ran her fingers over the smooth wood.

Every day after school, she would hurry home, eager to practice on the old, weathered cello her parents had found at her grandmother's house—the very same one her grandfather had played.

Many months later, it was time for the concert her music club had been practicing for. Her whole family was there, including her grandmother. She could see them in the second row and waved as she went over to her cello to make sure everything was as it should be.

Half an hour later, she was playing her cello for the whole auditorium to hear. Playing the cello for an audience was an experience unlike any she had ever had. With the cello rested against her chest, its wooden body vibrating, and the bow smooth and familiar in her hand, she loved how the instrument translated her emotions into sound.

As she followed the conductor's movements, her heart pounded, not from nerves, but from the rich and full sound the cello made. As she played, the music took over, and the audience seemed to narrow to the sound of the cello as the music flowed through her, as if the cello was alive with the rich warm sound—from sorrowful, heart-wrenching melodies to joyful, exuberant bursts.

Polly realized she wasn't just playing the cello—she was part of something much larger, something magical that had the power to move hearts and stir souls. She felt like she was stirring her grandfather's soul with her music. She hadn't felt this close to him since he'd passed, and she knew he was there with her, feeling the music. She felt the connection and looked out into the crowd to see her family and all her new friends. She knew that after all her searching, she had finally found her thing! Plus, she felt comfortable with her music AND her poetry writing, so she now had multiple things!

> *Polly's story teaches us that finding where you truly belong takes time, perseverance, and an open heart. Despite initial struggles and doubts, Polly discovered her passion for the cello, love of writing, and a connection to her family. Her journey reminds us that it's okay to explore and fail before finding what that truly makes us happy and feel at home.*

Conclusion

As you close this book, take a moment to reflect on the incredible journeys you've just experienced. Each story was a reminder of the unique and powerful qualities you also possess. You've seen how girls just like you were brave in the face of fear, kind in the midst of hardship, thoughtful when making tough decisions, creative when finding solutions to their problems, and unstoppable when chasing their dreams.

Remember, the strength, courage, and wisdom you admired in these characters are qualities that you already have and can tap into. Embrace new experiences, challenge assumptions, and step boldly beyond your comfort zone.

You can accomplish great things, overcome challenges, and make a difference in the world. Never forget how special and amazing you are. The possibilities are limitless, and your heart is your greatest guide.

As you go about your days, remember that you are powerful, you are resilient, and you are enough. Let these stories be a source of light, reminding you of the incredible girl you are inside. The world is waiting for your unique spark—go out and shine!

Conclusion

INSPIRING STORIES
FOR
AMAZING BOYS

Empowering Tales of Courage,
Confidence, and Kindness

Katie Wensley

Introduction

Psst... Want to know a secret?

There's something super cool inside this book: it's all about YOU!

Inspiring Stories for Amazing Boys is packed with ten awesome adventures, showing how boys just like you can be brave even when they're scared, kind even when they feel jealous, and do the right thing even when it's hard. From video game battles to tough days at school, these boys always find ways to keep going—and you will too!

You're already amazing just as you are! Life can get tricky sometimes, but you're much stronger than you think. By the time you finish this book, you'll feel ready to take on anything that comes your way!

Happy reading!

The Not-So-Superhero

"**N**oah! You're going to hurt yourself, buddy," eight-year-old Noah's mother called, worried her son might fall and bump his head. Noah didn't listen; he continued to race around the house.

"Look, mommy! Look! I'm the fastest boy in the world," he shouted while giggling and doing his very best to make his little legs go even faster. Skillfully, he avoided running into any furniture.

Noah was an intelligent boy with a big dream. He wanted to be a superhero, just like Superman, Batman, or one of the Avengers. After school, he never missed watching movies about superheroes and adored how people marveled at them. They were strong and brave—everything Noah wanted to be.

"Mom," he suddenly called, stopping himself by grabbing onto his mother's leg and trying to swipe a piece of fried chicken from a plate she was carrying. His mother chuckled and raised the plate out of his reach.

"Yes, darling?" she asked while passing him plates to set the dinner table.

"Mom, do you think if I practice enough, I might become like Superman too?" Noah asked curiously with a tilt of his head. Noah arranged the plates at the table while awaiting his mother's answer.

His mother stood with her hand stroking her chin and eyes pointed at the ceiling. She was thinking long and hard. Noah was growing excited to hear what she would say. He could hardly stand still, arms fidgeting away, and legs pacing about.

"I think you can," his mother finally confirmed with a nod of her head. She looked so sure of it that Noah became extremely happy. He cheered, spending the rest of the day running around to get faster and lifting his dad's gym bag to get stronger.

He ran to the mirror every so often and checked to see if he had grown muscles. Lifting his shirt, a frown formed on his lips as he saw no abs yet.

"Dad, do I look more muscle-y to you?" he asked hoping his father would see some difference in his physique.

His father looked over, eyes widening. He lifted the boy's arms and wiggled them around before lightly tapping the top of his head.

"You know what? I think you do, buddy!" he said. Noah cheered in excitement.

"Yes, yes, yes! I'm going to be a superhero soon, you know, dad? Like Superman! Or maybe even the Hulk." Noah's eyes lit up as he daydreamed about being a superhero, his imagination running wild.

His father, with a gentle smile and a stretch, let out a big yawn. "Being strong and fast is cool, but they aren't the only things that make you a superhero, buddy," he said, his voice calm and wise.

"Huh? What do you mean? All superheroes are super strong and super fast. Some of them fly too, but Mommy says I can't do that, and she doesn't want me trying either," Noah said with a pout, remembering the earlier conversation. His father chuckled, gently ruffling Noah's hair—something Noah never enjoyed. He sulked even more.

"You'll see, kiddo," his dad said with a wink. "Superheroes are all around us. You just have to keep your eyes wide open." He whispered the last bit dramatically, stretching his eyes wide in a goofy way. Noah couldn't help it— he erupted into laughter, the sound filling the room.

That night, Noah tossed and turned, replaying his father's words in his mind. What did he mean? Where were all the superheroes? Surely, he would have noticed if they were around! Eventually, his eyelids drooped, and little by little, he drifted into a peaceful sleep.

The next day at school, Noah could hardly pay attention. He kept imagining himself wearing a bright red cape that flew behind him. His hands were on his hips, and he held his head high, just like the superheroes he dreamed of.

"Alright, class, today we're going to do something a little different," Mr. Wilson, Noah's English teacher, announced, snapping Noah out of his daydream. "Let's talk about the heroes in our lives." Noah's eyes lit up— finally, he could talk about superheroes!

Noah couldn't make up his mind as he tried to pick his favorite superhero. Would it be Ironman? Maybe the classic Superman? Or someone speedy like The Flash?

"Oh man, how can I pick just one?" Noah whispered to his best friend, James.

"I can't choose either," James frowned as he tried to pick his own favorite hero.

The other children excitedly yelled out their favorite heroes.

"Aquaman is my favorite!" Pierre said as he made a swimming motion through the air.

"No no! Black Panther is the best!" Tom insisted, slamming his hands on his desk to draw attention.

"Ghostrider! Ghostrider! You can't do better than that," Mikayla shouted excitedly, waving her arms in the air. "He's got fire."

"Yes, I can, actually. Try beating Spiderman!" Lola pretended to shoot webs out of her hands.

The squeaky, excited voices filled the room, growing louder with every second. Kids were shouting out names, each trying to convince the others that their superhero was the best.

Noah wasn't about to be left out. He joined in, yelling a whole bunch of his favorite superhero names.

Mr. Wilson finally had to calm the class down. "You've got lots of ideas now, which is awesome. Pick your favorite superhero and write a short paragraph explaining why you chose them. Any questions?"

Noah grew curious. He raised his hand and Mr. Wilson called on him.

"Mr. Wilson, do you have a favorite superhero?" The class went so silent you might have been able to hear a pin drop. Mr. Wilson closed his eyes and smiled.

"Why, yes I do, actually," he nodded. My favorite superhero... is my mom."

"Woah! Your mom's a superhero? Can I meet her?" Noah exclaimed. Mr. Wilson chuckled.

"Well, she's a superhero in a way. She's my superhero," he said. Before anyone could ask more questions, he told them to start their assignment.

The classroom filled with groans and frustrated sighs, but Noah wasn't upset like the others. Instead, he felt confused, just like he had the night before when talking with his dad.

"Why can't I see these superheroes? I've never seen one before..." Noah thought sadly as he and James walked toward the school courtyard.

Suddenly, Noah saw Billy, the biggest kid in school. Billy, an older student known for bullying younger kids, was at it again, this time picking on tiny Madison from first grade. Noah, like most kids in school, was afraid of Billy and stood frozen in place as he watched the bullying unfold. A crowd of students gathered. Noah quickly searched the area for a teacher, but no one was there to help

Noah watched Billy pull on Madison's pigtails. He wanted to help, but fear held him back, leaving him feeling powerless. His heart pounded in his chest.

"Silly piggy," Billy called Madison, causing the little girl's eyes to water. She started sobbing uncontrollably.

Unexpectedly, a voice yelled, "Stop it, Billy! Leave Madison alone!"

The crowd of kids parted, allowing someone to move forward. Noah saw the brave student who had spoken. It was Amber Kim, rolling up in her wheelchair. Billy just laughed, but it wasn't a nice laugh.

Oh no! Amber is new to this school. She doesn't know how scary Billy can be. He's like a monster! Noah thought, his eyes growing huge, his palms getting sweaty with fear.

"What do you want, wheelchair?" Billy teased, his words making a few kids gasp. But Amber didn't even blink. She sat there calmly, looking up at him without saying a word. Billy shifted uncomfortably, not sure what to do next.

"You know, Billy, my mom tells me that bullies are only bullies because they've got lots of hurt and sadness in their hearts," Amber told him.

"Why should I care what your mom says, hmm?" Billy challenged her. He crossed his arms over his chest and tapped his foot.

"Well, my mom *is* a psychologist," she said, her fingers tapping the armrest of her wheelchair.

"A psycho? That sounds about right. You must have gotten it from her," Billy laughed.

The crowd of students shook their heads at Billy's mean comment, but no one dared to step forward. They didn't want trouble with Billy. The whispers continued among the students and they waited to see how things would unfold.

"Not psycho. Psychologist. When I was little, she explained it to me this way. She's a *feelings doctor* and takes care of people who feel hurt on the inside instead of the outside," Amber explained while wrapping her arms around her body and giving herself a squeeze. "So my mom's a genius."

Billy's face turned as red as a tomato. He was so angry, he didn't even notice Madison sneaking away to hide behind Amber's wheelchair. Stomping over to Amber, Billy raised his arm like he was going to hit her.

But Amber quickly put her hands up and shouted, "No, stop it, Billy!"

This time, Billy froze, scared that a teacher might have heard. He didn't want to get in trouble—his parents were very strict. He looked around nervously when Amber suddenly spoke up again.

"Billy, I'm sorry that you're feeling sad and mad. I'm here if you ever want to talk. But it's not okay to hurt other kids because of how you feel. You look silly when you bully people," Amber said calmly. Billy looked down, embarrassed—no one had ever talked to him like that before.

From where he stood, Noah noticed a few things. Billy looked like he felt a little bad about what he did. And Madison, along with everyone else, was looking at Amber with admiration. It reminded Noah of the way people look at Superman after he saves the day.

At that moment, Noah finally understood what his dad meant. Not all superheroes wear capes or fly or shoot lasers from their eyes. Some stay right here on the ground, and they can be friends or even strangers.

That night, Noah had a lot to share during dinner.

"It was so cool! Billy even said sorry after," Noah said, stuffing a big spoonful of mac and cheese into his mouth. His parents looked at each other and laughed.

"Is that right? So, do you see superheroes now?" his dad asked, wiping sauce from his mustache.

"You're right, dad. They're all around us. Everywhere," he informed his parents. With a big grin, he said, "I'm going to be a superhero just like Amber someday!"

> *Noah's story shows us that being a superhero isn't about having super strength or speed, but about standing up for what's right and being kind. Even though Amber wasn't big or powerful, she showed true courage by standing up to a bully and protecting Madison. This teaches us that real heroes, no matter how big or small they are, are the ones who help others, and that bravery comes from doing the right thing, even when it's hard.*

The Reckless Racer

The sun shone brightly over the small town of Elmwood Grove. It was here that 12 year old Evan could often be seen zipping past on his bright red bike.

Ever since he was a little boy, Evan has always loved bike races. He started out with an itty-bitty little tricycle that his parents gifted him on his fourth birthday. Then, he got a bicycle with training wheels. Eventually, those training wheels came off and Evan's passion for bike racing grew stronger than ever.

Everyone in town knew Evan. When people heard his name, they'd say, "Oh, that's the boy with the bike."

"The child has so much talent, don't you think, Geraldine?" his aunt had once said to his mother, watching him race around.

It was true! Evan, though still quite young, had somehow managed to teach himself all sorts of tricks. He could do a front and back wheelie and took great pride in it.

The more tricks Evan learned, the more he swelled with pride. People cheered for him, and he loved it. Soon, he started doing riskier and more dangerous stunts.

His mother tried to get him to stop. At first, she spoke gently, "Evan, sweetie, those stunts are really dangerous. I'm worried about you." She sat him down and explained how risky his tricks were.

Evan heard her, but he didn't listen. He rushed out the door that evening and showed off more stunts to his neighbors and friends. His riding became more and more unsafe.

As Evan's stunts got wilder, his mom's warnings got louder. "Evan Baxter, if you don't stop right now, you'll be grounded until you leave for college!" she yelled, her face filled with worry.

This got his attention. He rode his bike around safely for a while in the evenings. But there was no fun, no thrill to his days anymore.

Evan spent the whole week complaining to his mom, hoping she'd change her mind, but she didn't. He was unhappy and made sure she knew it by grumbling and not talking to her whenever they crossed paths.

Knock, knock, knock! Someone was at the front door.

"Who could that be?" his mom whispered as she dried her hands on her apron and opened the door. Standing there was Patricia, their neighbor, holding her tiny Chihuahua.

"Geraldine, I hope this isn't a bad time. I wanted to drop this off," Patricia said with a big smile, handing Evan's mom a flyer while scooping her dog up into her arms. The Chihuahua let out a squeaky bark.

"What's this?" Evan's mom asked, taking the flyer.

"It's a bike race! I thought Evan might be interested," Patricia said, leaning in like it was a secret. "Anyway, I've got to run. I've got a casserole in the oven."

"Take care!" his mom called as Patricia waved and hurried back to her house.

Evan, who had been eavesdropping the whole time, ran out and begged to join the race.

"You haven't even seen the details yet," his mom said, putting the flyer down neatly on the table and heading back to the kitchen.

Evan grabbed the flyer, his eyes scanning every word—except for the part about the $50 entrance fee.

"Mom, this looks amazing! It's on a weekend so I don't have to miss school either. Also, did you see this part?" he asked, pointing to a corner of the flyer. "Grand prize $200!"

"Did you see the entrance fee, though, sweetie?" his mom asked while intently dropping spices into the dish she was preparing.

E Evan groaned. "It's only $50, Mom. Please," he said, begging and listing every reason he could think of as to why he just had to join the race. His mom stayed quiet, listening.

"Fifty dollars is a lot of money for us right now, Evan. And there's no guarantee we'll win $200," she said. Evan's shoulders drooped, and his face fell. "But, I know how much you love racing, and you've been better about racing safely. Let's go ahead and get your name on the list!"

Evan's eyes went wide with surprise. "Really? You mean it, Mom?" he asked, barely able to believe it.

His mother nodded, smiling down at her son as she ruffled his hair. Evan cheered and jumped around with excitement, then hugged his mom tightly.

"But–" Evan's mother suddenly interrupted his celebration, "–you have to promise that you're not going to do anything dangerous." Her face turned serious. Evan gulped. His mom was usually kind and gentle, but she could be really scary when she needed to be.

"I promise," Evan said with a confident nod. Surely, he could hold off on the cool stunts for a while.

The race was a month away, and Evan spent every spare second practicing. He wanted nothing more than to win. Everyone knew him as "Lightning Evan," and losing would be way too embarrassing.

After school, he'd rush home, complete his homework, and run straight over to his red bike parked in the garage. He practiced at least an hour each day, sometimes even before school.

He also took great care of his bike, oiling the chains and keeping it bright and shiny for race day. "I'm keeping it squeaky clean so it'll look good in the pictures," he told his mother with a grin.

"The pictures?" she asked.

"Yeah! You know, the pictures people will take when I win! Maybe they'll put me in the newspaper!" Evan scratched the back of his head, already imagining his big victory.

He was sure he'd win, no question about it. There was no competition. Until one day, his classmates, Peter and Luna, told him something that made his legs shake for the first time.

"Did you hear about the new kid in the neighborhood?" Peter asked during lunch.

"No, who?" Evan said through a mouthful of tuna sandwich.

"He's a transfer student. Wait! There he is now!" Luna called while pointing at a tall boy with pale skin and short, straight hair.

"My mom says he's from Japan. I talked to him earlier, and he's really nice. His name's Yura. I bet you two would get along," Peter said.

"Oh? Why?" Evan asked.

"He's a bike racer too. You might see him at the race this weekend," Luna said

Evan got up, stuffed his hands in his pockets, and looked at Yura. He seemed nice with a big smile and hearty laugh. Lots of students crowded around him, listening to his stories from Japan—especially the ones about how he'd won so many bike races.

As the days passed, whenever Evan walked by, kids whispered about him in the hallway. The same thing happened in class, while waiting for the bus, and even when he went on his evening bike ride. Evan grew quieter, and a sick feeling started to grow in his stomach. He was more worried than he'd ever been.

What if I don't win? he thought, riding through the neighborhood, not paying attention. He almost knocked over poor Mrs. Fitzgerald, his ninety-year-old neighbor. She gave him a mean look, and he yelled out an apology, panicking.

That night, after dinner, Evan went straight to his room. He skipped his usual evening talks with his mom, saying he had homework to do. The race was the next day, and it was all anyone at school could talk about.

Evan became more determined than ever to win, and that's when he had his first bad idea. He decided to cheat. He stayed up late, under his blanket with a flashlight, pencil, and notebook, mapping out the race route.

But he knew a shortcut—at the corner right between Darby Street and Springhill Lane.

I'll never lose to anyone! He whispered to himself, voice full of determination and passion.

Whenever he heard his mom coming, he turned off the flashlight and pretended to be asleep. By 3 a.m., he had memorized the route, tossed the paper in the trash, and finally went to bed.

The day of the race finally came and everyone gathered at the starting line to see the contestants off. Peter and Luna were there to cheer for Evan. But Evan's eyes were fixed on Yura.

Yura was smiling and laughing with his friends while the other racers warmed up and checked their bikes one last time. Evan thought it would be nice to wish Yura good luck before the race, so he walked over to introduce himself.

"Hey, I'm Evan," he said with a smile. Yura turned around, beaming.

"Evan! I've heard a lot about you," Yura said, shaking his hand. "Good luck in the race!"

The happiness in Yura's voice made Evan second-guess his plan. Yura didn't seem like he cared about beating him—he was just having fun. Evan almost decided not to cheat. Almost.

"On your marks!" the official, Peter's dad, shouted into the megaphone. All the racers stood straight at the starting line, eyes focused on the road ahead.

"Get set!" Evan's heart pounded in his chest. This was really happening.

"Go!" With that, the entire line of racers sped off, their bikes disappearing in a flash. Behind them, the crowd cheered wildly. As Evan sped away, the sound got softer and softer and then wasn't there at all.

Evan was leading the race with the other racers far behind him. He felt his confidence come back and pedaled even faster. He swooshed through each turn and checkpoint effortlessly. His bike was handling perfectly.

All of a sudden, without warning, Yura zoomed past him with a polite, toothy. Evan leaned forward on his bike, pedaling faster than he ever had before. His legs were going numb, but he couldn't overtake Yura. Yura had soared far ahead.

Then, Evan remembered his plan. He scanned the bushes and trees, looking for the shortcut he had planned out the night before. Suddenly, he saw it!

Without a second glance, Evan turned off the main path and rode onto the trail. It was darker than he remembered, with thick bushes and roots sticking up everywhere. It felt strange and a little scary, but he kept going. All he could think about was winning.

Suddenly, a loud snap echoed through the woods and Evan found himself tumbling down a steep slope. He kept falling as he grabbed for roots and vines, but they broke in his hands. He felt dizzy as he tumbled down, and when he finally hit the ground, the world went black.

* * *

The next thing Evan heard was his mom crying and lots of voices he didn't recognize. He tried to open his eyes, but the light was too bright, so he quickly shut them again.

Slowly, he got used to the light and opened his eyes. He sat up and looked around an unfamiliar room. The first thing he did was search for his mom, who he found sleeping in a chair next to him.

"Mom," he called softly as she stirred awake.

"Oh, baby! You're finally awake!" she cried, jumping up and hugging him tightly.

"What happened, Mom? My legs hurt," he said, feeling confused. He cried out as a sharp pain shot through his knee.

"Don't move, sweetie. You took a tumble during the race and fell into a pit. Luckily, an old couple was walking by and saw you. That's how we found you. But you broke your leg."

Evan threw the blanket off and saw his right leg wrapped in a thick, white cast.

Evan felt his heart sink. Not only did he lose the race, but he wouldn't get to compete in any more races this season. He hung his head in sadness and shame. Tears streamed down his cheeks and he sniffled, trying to hold them back.

"I'm sorry, mom," he apologized, realizing how worried she must have been.

His mom didn't say anything right away, which made Evan think she was mad at him. Maybe she was, but she loved him even more. She leaned down and gave him a gentle kiss on the top of his head.

Evan looked up and saw her smiling. "I'm definitely upset that you did something so dangerous, but I think not being able to race is already a big enough punishment."

"I should've listened to you! You warned me not to do dangerous stuff, and now I can't even race my bike because I didn't listen to what you said!" Evan cried as he hugged his mom tightly.

"Well, let this be a lesson," his mom said softly. "We just want you to stay safe, sweetheart. That's why we give you advice, not to stop your fun, but to protect you."

Evan nodded and made a promise to himself. From now on, he would be more careful and follow the rules. Cool tricks might be fun, but they weren't worth getting hurt over.

> *Evan's story teaches us that sometimes our desire to win or impress others can lead to poor decisions. At first, Evan was determined to win the race, even if it meant cheating and taking dangerous risks. But when he got hurt, he realized that being safe and following the rules is much more important than winning at any cost. This story reminds us that our safety and well-being should always come first, and that shortcuts can lead to unexpected consequences.*

The Littlest Explorer

"Alright kids, has everyone got their permission slips?" Mr. Wilson called from the front of the class, waving a piece of paper in the air.

"Yes!" the students called in a sing-song way, their little fingers gripping tightly onto similar looking papers.

The kids of class 2A were due to go on a camping trip the following weekend. It was a two-day, one-night stay in one of Florida's camping forests.

The children were absolutely thrilled, as most eight-year-olds would be. Many of them had never been camping before and the ones that had talked a great deal about it. Everyone was grinning from ear to ear, except little Marcus Ng.

Marcus adjusted his thick glasses on the bridge of his nose and looked around. He had never gone anywhere without his parents and wasn't sure if he wanted to now. He frowned, his hands hidden inside his oversized sweater.

"I can't wait! Maybe we'll see bears! The big white ones!" Noah shouted, making his fingers into claws and growling at his friends.

"Those are called polar bears, Noah. And I doubt we'll be seeing any in these parts. They live in the Arctic," Mr. Wilson chuckled as he explained.

"What about vampires? My cousin said she saw lots of vampires flying around when she went camping!" Gabe asked. Mr. Wilson looked up at him and burst out laughing.

"I think she was teasing you," Mr. Wilson said, still smiling.

"No no! She said they were flying and they were the size of fat cats," Gabe insisted.

"Well those might have been vampire bats. Not vampires. In my thirty-two years on this Earth, I've never known anyone who came about a vampire," Mr. Wilson said with a shake of his head. "Now stop scaring the rest of the class."

Marcus wasn't all too fond of big white bears or vampires—whether they were bats or not! He sunk down in his seat and thought of ways he might be able to skip out on the camping trip.

"Mr. Wilson?" Marcus called with his hand only half in the air.

"Yes, Marcus?"

"If we get sick the day of the camp, will we still have to go?" he asked, thinking of excuses but knowing full well that his parents would never pass on the chance for him to be social and gain some real world experience.

Mr. Wilson put his book down and sat at the front of his desk with one eyebrow higher than the other. "Are you planning on being sick that day?" he questioned the nervous boy.

Marcus fidgeted with the sleeves of his sweater and mumbled a quiet no before slumping down and putting his head on his desk. Mr. Wilson smiled warmly.

"It'll be alright, Marcus. You'll see. Once we get there, it's going to be fun," Mr. Wilson said, trying to cheer him up, but Marcus wasn't so sure. He was still worried about things like bears and scary creatures.

The rest of the day flew by with more talk about the camping trip. Marcus walked through the hallways and heard Melissa talking about wanting to meet Bigfoot. Another classmate, Sonya, said she heard they were only going to be given earthworms during mealtime. The worst rumor was from Jacob, who said that teachers would leave naughty kids in the jungle and head back to school without them!

The bus ride home was no better. Noah said that the kids that went on the school trip last year all got eaten by mummies.

"Aren't mummies supposed to be in Egypt?" Sonya asked while scratching her head.

"Yeah. So?" Noah retorted.

"So why would they be on our camping trip?"

Noah gulped, looking nervous. He didn't have an answer.

"May... maybe the mummies took a plane here?" Marcus stuttered.

"Oh, don't be silly, Marcus. *Everyone* knows mummies aren't allowed on airplanes!" Gabe called from the back of the bus. "Besides, they don't even have mouths to eat us."

Marcus didn't want to join the conversation anymore. In his mind, he had decided that going on this camping trip meant that he would meet Bigfoot and be eaten by mummies. He was absolutely shaking in fear.

When Marcus got off the bus, things didn't get any better. He spent the rest of the day hiding in his room, crying in the shower, and refusing to tell his mom anything.

Worried about Marcus's strange behavior, Marcus's mom sent his older brother, Peter to try to find out what might be bothering him.

"Peter, could you check on your brother?" she asked, resting her chin on her hand, her eyebrows furrowed with worry.

Peter didn't ask any questions. The moment his mother told him about his younger brother, he went straight to Marcus's room, knocked three times, and waited.

Knock, knock, knock.

No answer. Peter knocked again, this time louder.

KNOCK, KNOCK, KNOCK!

Still no answer. Peter pressed his ear against the cold door and heard quiet sobbing.

"Marcus! I'm coming in!" Peter called as he opened the door and stepped into the dark room.

He switched on the lights and noticed streaks of tears staining Marcus's face. Peter rushed over and hugged his little brother, and Marcus held onto him, crying. Peter patted Marcus' back gently to calm him down.

When Marcus was only sniffling, Peter pulled away and asked, "What's wrong? Is someone bothering you at school?"

Marcus didn't say anything. He reached into his bag and handed Peter the permission slip for the camping trip.

Peter took it, read it, and his eyes lit up. "Oh! You're going on the school trip? I remember my trip when I was your age! It was four years ago, and—"

"You went on the school trip?" Marcus interrupted, looking surprised.

Peter nodded. "Of course I did. It was fun!" he said, smiling as he remembered his own trip.

"How come the mummies didn't eat you?" Marcus asked, tilting his head in confusion.

Peter looked shocked. "What do you mean?" he asked.

"Well, Noah said there were mummies that flew all the way from Egypt to eat us. And then Sonya said we'd have to eat worms for dinner!" Marcus said, starting to cry again, but stopped when Peter started to chuckle.

"No, nothing like that happens at camp, Marcus. Your teachers are going to take very good care of you. And after dinner, you get to sit around a campfire and roast marshmallows. No one's going to make you eat worms," Peter giggled.

"Really?" Marcus asked. He should've been happy but he was still uncertain.

"You know? I've never really known you to be scared of these sorts of things. Maybe you're just anxious about going on the trip?" Peter asked, looking closely at his brother.

"An–shios? What's that?" Marcus tried to sound it out and Peter giggled as he patted his head.

"Anxious," Peter repeated slower this time. "It's a funny feeling you get in your tummy sometimes when you're scared or nervous."

Marcus made an "O" shape with his mouth but didn't say anything. He thought about it while Peter waited. After a moment, Marcus nodded slowly.

"I think I am—anxious," he looked to his brother. Peter nodded. "I've never been away from you, mom, and dad before. Not for *two whole days!* And what if a bear does eat me?" Marcus cried.

Peter smiled softly at him, patting his head. "You're not going to get eaten by anything. I felt the same way on my first camping trip too. I missed you, mom, and dad even before I left. But you know how I got over it?" Peter whispered like it was a secret. Marcus shook his head.

"I brought a tiny notebook along and wrote down everything I wanted to tell you guys back home."

Marcus leaned back and thought about it. It was a good idea! Writing in a notebook would help him feel better. He relaxed for awhile as Peter told him stories about his own camping trip.

Finally, with a big smile on his face, Marcus walked downstairs with his brother and gave his mother the permission slip. She was more than happy to sign it.

Marcus and his parents went shopping for everything Marcus would need for camp and didn't forget to get him a small purple notebook. It was tiny enough to fit in his pocket, with a pen attached by a string of purple beads.

The day of the camping trip came finally came, and Marcus felt a little nervous during the bus ride to the camp site. He pulled out his notebook and scribbled in messy handwriting: *The bus ride is a bit scary, but I like hearing the stories people are telling. I'm sitting next to my best friend, Hunter. I miss you mom, dad, and Peter!*

He put his notebook away, and soon they arrived at the campsite. The games and activities started right away, and Marcus made sure to write everything down:

I learned how to put up a tent. Mr. Wilson says that I'm a natural. I also found a lost compass.

Noah went looking for bears but found a squirrel instead. He scared it. It was hurt so we took care of it and named it Chocolate because of its fluffy, brown tail.

I caught a fish today! Just like dad! It scared me a little, so I don't think I'll be going fishing again.

Melissa told a campfire story about big spiders in the forest waiting to get us. But I wasn't scared at all!

Pretty soon, his notebook was filled with all sorts of stories and he couldn't wait to get home to share them. His friends liked his notebook idea and even tried to write their stories on leaves. Mr. Wilson praised Marcus for the excellent idea. Marcus grinned and said, "It was all my brother's idea."

Before the trip ended and they had to leave, Marcus crouched down next to a big rock and got his notebook out for one last entry.

It said: *I had lots of fun! Thanks, Peter! I can't wait to get home and tell you everything. I miss you all. See you soon! Love, Marcus.*

> *Marcus's story shows us that it's normal to feel nervous about trying new things, but sometimes facing our fears can lead to great experiences. At first, Marcus was scared of going camping and imagined all sorts of things going wrong. But with the support of his brother, Peter, and by writing down his thoughts in a notebook, Marcus overcame his worries and ended up having a fun adventure. This story shows us that when we face our fears and try new things, we often discover that they aren't as scary as we thought—and we can even have fun along the way.*

The Jealous Friend

Crestview Elementary was famous for many things. There was their taekwondo team, their junior badminton players, and their melodious choir. But the one thing it was most famous for was its soccer team.

Juan was one of the players on the team. He joined the team two years ago when he was only eight years old.

He had actually started showing a passion for soccer from an even younger age. The moment he could walk, he started kicking things around. So his mother bought him a blue rubber ball that was made for kids. Juan loved it with all his heart. He never went anywhere without his favorite blue ball.

One day at the park, he saw a group of high school boys kicking and chasing after a ball, a lot like he did. He stopped playing, sat on the grass, and watched intently while the older boys played. His keen interest and curiosity didn't go unnoticed by his parents.

Later, he asked his parents what those boys were playing and found out it was a sport called soccer. From that day onwards, Juan was passionate about soccer.

Today, Juan had just finished playing another big game for his school, and Crestview Elementary had won! Everyone was cheering—the students, the parents, and the teachers. But Juan didn't feel happy. His face was red, and not just from running around. The cheering went on and no one noticed that he was upset. Juan became more and more cross. His face twisted into an unpleasant frown.

As the team gathered, the coach and other players praised Juan's best friend, Ricardo, for scoring the winning goal.

"Good job, Ricardo!" Coach called while they walked up to the benches.

"That was amazing!" one of their teammates cheered.

"What would we have done without you, Ricardo? That shot was legendary!" the team's goalkeeper shouted happily.

Juan and Ricardo had been best friends since they were still in diapers. They always played together, and as they grew up, they started sharing the same hobbies. At first, Juan loved it because they could spend even more time together after school. But today, Juan wasn't happy at all.

You see, Juan was the first to love soccer and Ricardo only started playing after Juan introduced him to it. Juan taught Ricardo many of the tricks he knew. Now, watching Ricardo score the winning goal, something new and uncomfortable bubbled up in Juan's stomach.

"Juan, Juan! Did you see that? Did you see how I scored the goal?" Ricardo called out while jogging towards his best friend. Juan gave him an unpleasant glare.

"Yeah, I saw. You used the move I taught you." Juan said unenthusiastically, not even looking at Ricardo.

"Oh, right! I guess I did. Thanks, amigo!" Ricardo said, moving closer to pat Juan on the back, but Juan stepped away. Ricardo's smile faded, and his eyebrows lowered in confusion.

Coach noticed Juan's angry face and asked, "What's wrong, Juan?"

By now, other players had gathered around. Ricardo was silent, trying to figure out why Juan was so upset. Everyone was confused.

All of a sudden, Juan shouted angrily, "I was supposed to score the winning goal. Me! Not you!" he yelled while pointing a finger at Ricardo. Ricardo was shocked and didn't say anything. He didn't understand why his friend was so angry.

"But we won, I don't understand why you're so mad," Ricardo whispered.

"That was supposed to be my winning kick. Not yours. I passed the ball to you!" Juan yelled in frustration. Tears welled in his eyes.

"Exactly. You passed me the ball, so I kicked it into the goal and we won," Ricardo explained, still confused.

Juan got more furious. He clenched his small fists by his side and shouted, "You were supposed to pass it back to me. That was my winning kick and you stole it!" And with that, Juan ran off the field, upset.

He kept running until his legs got tired. When he finally stopped, he realized he had run halfway home. As he walked the rest of the way, he kept thinking about how angry he was at Ricardo. *How dare he score the winning goal when I'm the one who introduced him to soccer!*

Juan thought of all the ways he wanted to hate Ricardo. But suddenly, memories of all the fun he and Ricardo had shared came back to him. Slowly, his anger started to fade, and he began to feel something else—guilt.

He was starting to feel bad for how he acted. He didn't even congratulate Ricardo on his victory, and he knew he ruined the team's celebration. He felt very ashamed of himself. He was also worried he had lost his best friend.

When he got home, he took a deep breath in and decide to talk to his parents. He always went to them for advice when he didn't know what to do. They always knew just what to say.

"Mom...Dad," he called nervously. His parents, who had just gotten home, looked at him. Juan suddenly felt more nervous than before. He wasn't sure how they would react—would they be upset? Or disappointed?

"Juan! Is the game over already? How was it?" his mother asked, clapping her hands with excitement.

"I bet your team won, right?" his father asked confidently.

Juan nodded weakly but didn't look up to meet his parents' eyes. He didn't cheer or ask for a snack like he usually did after winning a game. Instead, he just stood there, frowning and avoiding eye contact.

"Something happened after the game, and I want--" Juan started, but a knock at the door interrupted him.

"Hold on, sweetie," his mom said as she went to answer the door. Juan stood in silence and fidgeted with his fingers. He didn't know how to tell his parents without sounding like a bully.

"Juan, there you are, bud! I've been searching all over for you," a familiar gruff voice called from behind him. Juan turned to see Coach, who looked relieved.

"What's going on?" Juan's father asked as he walked over from the table.

"Juan had a little argument with Ricardo after the game and ran off," Coach explained. "We got worried when we couldn't find him."

"With Ricardo? But they're such good friends," Juan's mother said, surprised.

Coach looked over at Juan and raised his eyebrows as if saying, *do you want to tell them or should I?* Juan thought for a second and took another deep breath.

"I got mad at Ricardo during the game. He was supposed to pass the ball to me so I could score the winning goal, but he scored it himself instead. Everyone was praising him and cheering his name," Juan explained.

His parents listened quietly, and his mom knelt down to his level, rubbing soothing circles on his back. "Go on, sweetheart," she said softly.

"I just didn't like it that he joined the team because of me, but now he's in the spotlight, and I can't do anything for the team," he admitted through pouted lips while fighting back tears.

The adults looked at each other and stayed silent for a moment, trying to understand the situation. They thought for a long time, thinking carefully about what to say. Coach finally broke the silence.

"Juan, you know you're a fantastic player, right? And that the team is lucky to have you?" Juan shrugged.

Coach then continued, "Most people think that the only players who make a difference on the team are the strikers. But you're smart. You know soccer is more than that. What do you think about the other positions on the field?"

Juan thought about it. He pictured all the players and what they did during the game.

"The striker is important to score goals. But other positions are important too. The goalkeeper keeps our opponents from scoring a goal in our goalpost. The defense tries to steal the ball from the other team so they can't score a goal at all. Everyone has a purpose on the field." As he explained, he realized that he had it all wrong. It wasn't just one person who made them win—it was teamwork.

"There's no 'I' in team, son," his dad said, and Juan nodded.

"What about Ricardo? I yelled at him really badly earlier. What if he doesn't want to be my friend anymore? I don't think he's ever going to want to talk to me again."

Juan's mom hugged him tightly. "Don't worry, sweetie," she said. "I'm sure Ricardo will understand, but you need to apologize first."

When Monday came, Juan knew it was his chance to fix things. He walked around the school looking for Ricardo, but he wasn't waiting by the lockers like usual. Juan started to feel even more guilty and nervous about talking to him.

Just as the bell rang, Juan spotted Ricardo walking into their first class—English with Mr. Hendrick, who was always a few minutes late. Juan saw this as his chance to clear things up with Ricardo.

"Hey, Ricardo," Juan said, sitting down next to him. Ricardo looked a bit shocked but said hello back. They sat quietly for a moment, neither of them knowing what to say.

Juan was the one who broke the silence. "Ricardo, I'm sorry for how I acted the other day. I don't know what came over me. I guess I was a bit frustrated, that's all."

Ricardo thought for a second. Then, he smiled at Juan. "It's okay, it was a mistake. I understand."

The apology went smoothly, and soon the boys were back to laughing and joking around like usual.

Juan didn't forget the lesson he had learned. He started trying out different positions on the soccer field and discovered that he was really good at defense. He wasn't jealous of his teammates' wins anymore because he knew that a win for the team was a win for everyone.

He realized that working together and supporting his friends was what really mattered. Winning as a team felt a lot better than winning alone.

> *Juan's story shows us that it's easy to feel jealous when someone else gets recognition, but true friendship and teamwork mean celebrating each other's successes. Juan learned that it wasn't about who scored the winning goal—it was about how everyone played a part in the victory. By realizing that every player on the team is important, Juan discovered that winning together feels better than focusing on individual achievements. This reminds us to support and cheer for our friends, knowing that their success is a win for everyone.*

The Careless Student

"Go, go, go! To your left!" Jay called out in exasperation.

"Your left or my left?" Ben yelled back in confusion and panic.

"We have the same left, Ben!" Jay yelled back.

The pair of eleven-year-olds had arrived home from school and sat themselves down to play a series of video games. They started with *Mario Kart*, then moved on to *Call of Duty*.

It was almost dinner time. Ben had mentioned a few times that they had piles of homework to do for tomorrow, but Jay wasn't worried. He never worried about homework.

"Ben, your mom just called," Jay's mom said from the kitchen as she peeled potatoes for dinner. "She said to let you know that if you aren't back in the next fifteen minutes, she won't let you visit Jay after school anymore."

Ben gasped and scrambled to his feet, tossing the game controller to the side and rushing out. He yelled a quick goodbye to Jay as he rushed out the door and reminded him not to forget about his homework.

Jay pretended he didn't hear his friend and carried on playing. His mother—who had warned him at least three times to get started on his homework—was growing more and more frustrated. This had become the routine in their house.

Jay always came home from school, grabbed a quick snack, and started playing video games. His mother constantly nagged at him to do his homework and study for his tests, but he never listened.

"I don't *need* to study, mom. You know I'm a quick learner," Jay would say when his mom sent him to his room to study before a big test.

When she asked him to do his homework, he'd reply, "Don't worry, Mom. I'll get to it. It's super easy."

Jay was extremely confident because he always managed to get decent grades, so he didn't think he needed to change. But his mom kept reminding him that luck wouldn't always be on his side.

"You know the story of the hare and the tortoise, don't you, Jay? Well, just remember that even though the hare was definitely supposed to win that race, he lost to the tortoise because of his overconfidence."

Jay yawned and barely listened.

On the bus the next morning, Jay had his homework on his lap. He was only beginning to get it done. Ben glanced from his seat and saw what Jay was doing.

"I reminded you to do it *yesterday*," Ben muttered with a disappointed shake of his head.

"Yeah, but remember," Jay paused dramatically. "I'm a genius," he added, tapping his pencil against his head.

It was difficult to write down his answers because of the bumpy bus ride, but eventually, he finished.

"Done!" he announced while stuffing the paper into his school bag and tossing it to the side. He shut his eyes and leaned back in his seat while Ben stared at him.

"You really finished? It took me an hour to do all of it," Ben said.

From the seat in front of them, another one of their classmates, who overheard their conversation, agreed. And so did the girl beside her. They were amazed at how quickly Jay managed to finish the homework.

Jay just grinned. He always scored decent grades while submitting last minute work and not studying at all. So he felt like there was no need to study and put in any extra effort if he was just going to do well in the class anyway.

Their first lesson of the day was a science lesson. The students handed in their homework to Mr. Turner, who said they would be starting a new topic—cells.

Most of the students were really interested in the lesson. They took notes and tried their best to draw the plant cell like Mr. Turner did on the board. They struggled to understand at first but eventually did, and lots of questions were asked and answered.

Jay, on the other hand, was busy doodling video game characters and only half listening. He used to pay attention in class, but lately, since he'd been getting good grades without much effort, he thought fifth-grade subjects were too easy for him.

"The mitochondria is also known as the..." Mr. Turner paused to allow the students to answer the question.

"...powerhouse of the cell!" the majority yelled in unison while some mumbled it under their breath. Jay was the only one who hadn't answered. He didn't even hear the question. Mr. Turner noticed but didn't say anything because the bell rang, and everyone rushed off to their next class.

"I'll have your midterms and homework graded by tomorrow!" Mr. Turner called after the students.

The next day, Jay looked terrible. He kept nodding off in class, had dark circles under his eyes, and his skin looked pale. His hair was a mess too. He was exhausted.

"What happened to you?" Ben asked as he took a seat next to Jay.

Jay beamed at him and explained, "I was building a new house in Minecraft."

He went on to explain every detail of the pretend house. He also talked about how he got a new pet wolf in the game.

"A wolf? I didn't know you could do that in Minecraft," Ben said, taking his books out before Mr. Turner came in.

"Of course you didn't. I know because I'm a genius," Jay said, tapping a pencil on his head. "I just gave them some bones I found in the game and..." Jay kept talking, but Ben stopped listening.

Most of the students—except for Jay—were really nervous because Mr. Turner was going to hand back their midterm test grades.

Ben was tapping his foot absent-mindedly, Evelyn was humming a tune, and Poppy was making little origami cranes. Everyone had their own way of staying calm, but Jay was getting annoyed.

"He's only giving us back our test results, but you're all acting like the dentist is coming in to yank out a tooth," Jay grumbled.

Poppy turned around, annoyed. "Some of us studied really hard for this test. Of course we're nervous, Jay," she snapped at him.

Amir was frowning, too. "Yeah, not all of us were born geniuses," he said. Jay wasn't bothered at all. He shrugged and continued doodling on his paper.

"Good morning, class!" Mr. Turner called as he walked in. Everyone fixed themselves to their seats and stiffly waited as he passed out the tests. The room buzzed with excitement as students got their scores.

"Yes! I got an A!" Poppy shouted, high-fiving Ben, who also got an A.

"I got a B!" Evelyn said proudly. She usually struggled in Science, so she was happy with her grade.

Eventually, Jay's name was called and he strolled to the front to collect his results. Mr. Turner folded the paper in half as he handed it to him, which was strange because he didn't do that for anyone else. Back at his seat, Jay opened the paper.

His heart sank. A big F was written in bright red ink next to a short instruction: *See me after class.* He quickly folded the paper again, but William, who sat behind him, had already seen.

"Hey, did you fail, Jay?" William said loudly, making sure the whole class heard.

Everyone turned to look at Jay. Feeling embarrassed, he pulled his hoodie over his head and stared down at his desk for the rest of the class.

After the bell rang, Jay dragged his feet to Mr. Turner's desk. "Ah, Jay. Just the person I wanted to see," he said, still searching for something in a box next to his desk. His face twisted into a curious one as he felt around.

"Why did you fail me, Mr. Turner?" Jay asked, upset. He had never gotten anything lower than a B-minus before.

Jay flipped the test and realized he had missed an entire page of questions. He hadn't even seen them. Worse, when he checked the questions he *did* answer, most of them were wrong. His head spun, and he sat down in a nearby chair, confused.

"I see you've only just checked your answers?" Mr. Turner asked. Jay nodded, his eyes still staring at the big F at the top of his test.

"How did this happen?" Jay mumbled to himself. Mr. Turner suddenly started quizzing Jay.

"Jay, what's the fourth color of the rainbow?"

Jay thought for a while, recalling the pattern in his head. *Red, orange, yellow, green.* "It's green," he answered.

"Good, and what's the process called that enables ice to change to water?" the teacher asked.

"Ice to water? That's called melting," Jay answered more quickly.

"Alright, one last question, a snake is classified as a..." he looked at Jay intently with one eyebrow raised.

"A reptile. What does this have to do with anything, Mr. Turner?" Jay asked, gripping his test paper tightly. The teacher frowned.

"Jay, those are the same questions from the test that you got wrong. But you know the answers! You made careless mistakes."

Jay's mouth dropped open as he looked back at his test. It was true. For the rainbow question, he had written down orange. For the ice-to-water question, he had written freezing instead of melting. And for the snake question, he had written amphibian instead of reptile.

"You're right. I do know the answers... They're all careless mistakes," Jay realized with a gasp.

Mr. Turner patted Jay on the shoulder. "Have you been distracted lately? Sometimes, even when your body is here, your mind can be somewhere else. That can lead to mistakes."

Jay thought for a second, then groaned. "I was playing a new video game the night before, and it was so cool. During the test, I couldn't get it out of my head. The only thing I kept thinking about was how excited I was to get done with school, go home, and start playing the game again."

Mr. Turner didn't scold Jay or get mad. Instead, he pulled out a book called *Time Management for Beginners* and handed it to him. Jay took it quietly, flipping through the pages. When he was done, he looked up at Mr. Turner with curiosity.

"Believe it or not, I had the same problem when I was your age," Mr. Turner said. "A teacher gave me this book and told me it would change my life. Now, Jay, I want to give it to you."

Jay felt like he might cry but held it back. He stood up straight and nodded to Mr. Turner. It was a silent promise that he would change his habits and try to be more responsible.

Something about the confidence in Mr. Turner's eyes made Jay *want* to change his ways. It felt nice to have someone believe in him.

At home, Jay got a talking-to from his parents about the bad grade, but he accepted it. He understood that it was a consequence of his own actions. Later that night, his mom found him asleep earlier than usual. Placed neatly on his desk was a new daily schedule he created out of markers and highlighters. Next to it was the book Mr. Turner had given him.

Over the next month, Jay changed a lot. He still played video games to relax, but he limited it to just one hour a day—even on weekends! Instead, Jay spent more time studying, helping around the house, and finding new hobbies. He was very careful about following his schedule and even carried it in his folder wherever he went.

It was time to get their final exam results. Just like before, Mr. Turner called out everyone's name one by one. Just like before, Mr. Turner called out everyone's names one by one. The longer Jay's name wasn't called, the more worried he became.

Could it be possible that I failed again? He thought sadly.

"And last but not least, give a big round of applause for our tiny legend, Jay!" Mr. Turner lifted his test paper up and a big A+ was written at the top. Everyone clapped and congratulated him.

"Congratulations, Jay!" Ben said with a pat on Jay's back.

"Thank you, everyone. And thank you, Mr. Turner, for believing in me."

Jay kept the old test with the failing grade stored neatly in his room. He also pinned up the new test with his top score right next to it. The grades were a reminder to him that putting in effort, discipline, and doing the right thing would always lead to better results.

Jay's story teaches us that overconfidence and neglecting our responsibilities can lead to unexpected consequences. At first, Jay thought he could succeed without putting in effort, but when he failed his test, he realized that even smart people make mistakes when they don't focus or prepare. By learning the importance of time management and discipline, Jay turned his habits around and succeeded. This story reminds us that success isn't just about talent; it's about hard work and dedication.

The Recipe Book

Diego could hardly wait for five o'clock. He paced around the living room, sometimes walking into the kitchen and then back out. He had been doing this for half an hour.

"Just a few more minutes, Diego. We'll get cooking in just a bit," his grandmother said with a warm smile while she rocked on her rocking chair. Her hands were busy crocheting a colorful sweater.

Diego dropped to the floor with a thump. He whined about wanting to start cooking now. His grandmother smiled as she listened to him complain, which eventually turned into him telling stories.

"Joshua Wong said that he's going to bring a type of noodle that's famous in China. He's also going to teach us how to use chopsticks," Diego said, sticking out his tongue as he concentrated on trying to use his pretend chopsticks.

"Oh?" his grandmother said, amused.

"Yeah! And Raj is bringing something called Chapati. He says it's a flat bread made from flour that's cooked on a pan. Grandma, did you know people in India sometimes eat with their hands?"

"Yes, I did," his grandmother said. "I've had friends from India, and I've tried it myself. The flavors are delicious. So, what are you going to bring for Multicultural Week, Diego?"

He thought for a moment. There were so many things he wanted to bring, but each student was only allowed one dish. Finally, he made up his mind.

"How about salsa? It's easy to make and I could bring chips! We've got chips don't we grandma?" he asked with bright, hopeful eyes.

"Yes, dear, we do. I picked up some white corn chips at the store earlier. Why don't you go get the salsa ingredients out?"

Diego was ecstatic. He rushed to the kitchen and carefully got the ingredients out of the fridge. For a nine-year-old, Diego was surprisingly interested in cooking and knew exactly what to do, thanks to his grandmother, who had taught him ever since he was little.

Diego got out fresh tomatoes, onions, jalapeño peppers, cilantro, garlic, and lime. Since he wasn't allowed to use grown-up knives, he waited for his grandmother to bring his special kid-safe kitchen tools.

A few minutes later, his grandmother joined him, and they started chopping, dicing, and cooking the ingredients together. It was a fun time. They talked about their day and almost forgot the salsa on the stove, but they laughed about it.

The next morning, they took the salsa out of the fridge and heated it up before Diego brought it to school. He was so excited and kept telling his friends about the dish.

"It's usually spicy but grandma and I made sure to make it mild today since I didn't bring drinks," he informed his friends.

Everyone couldn't wait to taste the different dishes on the table. The bowls and plates were still covered, but the delicious smells made their mouths water.

"Alright, kids! Let's open up our dishes, shall we?" Miss Valerie called out cheerfully with a clap.

The kids rushed to the table, pulling the lids off their containers. The room filled with amazing smells, and everyone got even more excited.

"Mm...it smells delicious! Can we start tasting the dishes now, Miss?" Mary asked. The kids around her nodded ferociously.

Miss Valerie chuckled and said, "Hold on there. Let's get you guys to introduce your dishes. How about we start with–" she paused and scanned the eager little faces and decided, "–Diego?"

"Yes, Miss!" Diego said, pulling his salsa closer. "My dish is called salsa. It's made from tomatoes—"

"Ew! I hate tomatoes," Suzie interrupted. Diego was surprised but continued.

"It also has lime, onion—"

"That sounds horrible!" Joshua said while pinching his nose.

"I'm not eating that," Gemma looked at the salsa strangely. "It's too red."

"Well, you're supposed to eat it with chips. I brought some," Diego said, but before he could pull out the chips, the kids started protesting.

Miss Valerie had to calm everyone down and told them not to be mean. But the damage was done. Diego felt terrible and embarrassed that everyone was making fun of how his salsa smelled and looked.

A few kids were curious and wanted to try it, but after hearing the teasing, they decided to eat other food instead. By the end of the day, Diego's salsa was completely untouched except for a few bites he ate himself.

When Diego got home, he was really upset. His grandmother noticed and asked, "What's wrong, Diego?"

Diego, who had been holding back his feelings, burst into tears. "Abuela, it was awful! The kids made fun of my salsa, and no one ate it!" he cried as his grandmother hugged him. She frowned.

"Don't worry about what they said, okay? Kids can be mean sometimes," she said, trying to comfort him. Eventually, Diego started to calm down.

"I don't understand. They didn't even try it yet. Why would they make fun of it?" Diego said while blowing his nose into a tissue.

"Sometimes people need time to accept something new. They aren't used to it yet, but maybe one day they'll start liking it," his grandmother explained.

Diego had an idea. He didn't want his classmates to miss out on how delicious Mexican food could be. So, he and his grandmother made a plan.

The next Saturday, they woke up early and went to the store to buy lots of ingredients.

When they got back, his grandmother started calling the parents of Diego's classmates and invited them over for Sunday afternoon.

Plenty of kids could make it, so Diego got to work, looking through cookbooks and watching video tutorials. He had special dishes in mind and wanted to make them himself.

Sunday afternoon arrived, and one by one, Diego's classmates arrived at his grandmother's house. They loved how cozy it felt and the smell of fresh roses in the air.

"Your grandma has a lovely home, Diego," Suzie said while hugging a fluffy pillow Diego's grandmother made.

"Is this your cat? He's so cute! What's his name?" Joshua asked while petting a snow-white cat that purred happily.

"His name is Gato, but he's not the reason I invited you all here today," Diego said with a grin. "Follow me to the sink, everyone!"

Eight kids followed Diego through an archway into the sparkling clean kitchen. The countertops and floors shined. Diego told everyone to wash their hands and grab a plate.

They did as they were told, looking both excited and a little confused. Diego began giving instructions.

"You'll see some corn husks on the plate. Take one, like I'm doing, and put it in front of you," he demonstrated. The kids followed along. "Now, take some of the dough that my grandma and I made and put it at the top of the corn husk."

Next, the kids chose their fillings, which included shredded chicken, fish, beans, and even mozzarella cheese. The last step was to fold the corn husks, and they were done! After folding two tamales each, they handed them to Diego's grandmother, who was ready to steam them.

The kids were still a little confused, but they were having so much fun that no one minded. The kitchen was filled with laughter and joy as they followed Diego's instructions.

When everything was done, Diego's grandmother gathered them in the dining room and, with a big smile, served the steamed tamales they had made along with a green dipping sauce.

The kids were excited to see their creations and started eating right away. From the first bite to the last, they couldn't stop praising how delicious the food was.

"Oh, I wish we had made more!" Suzie said.

"Yeah! This is delicious, Diego. Thank you," Joshua said with a mouth full of food.

"I'm glad you like them. The first dish we made is called tamales, and the second one is guacamole. They're both traditional Mexican foods," Diego explained.

The room went silent. Everyone looked at each other with wide eyes, still chewing.

"I'm sorry, Diego. I didn't know Mexican food would taste this good," Gemma said, lowering her head.

"Yeah, I'm sorry too. I thought it looked different from what I usually eat, so I was worried it wouldn't taste good," Suzie added.

Eventually, everyone started apologizing. It brought a big smile to Diego's face and an even wider one to his grandmother's. It felt great to know that once the children tried the food, they loved it!

For the rest of the time, the kids asked all sorts of questions about Mexican food and its history, and Diego and his grandmother were happy to answer.

From that day on, Diego and his friends made one rule: *Never turn down anything before trying it, because you might end up liking it.*

Diego was happy he shared his culture with his friends. He realized there was nothing to be ashamed of and that sometimes people make fun of things that are different. And that was okay! If he was proud of his heritage, no one could make him feel bad about it.

Diego's story shows us the value of being open-minded and the importance of sharing and celebrating our cultures. At first, his classmates judged his salsa without even trying it, but when Diego gave them another chance to taste his food, they realized how much they loved it. This teaches us that we shouldn't reject something just because it's different or unfamiliar. By embracing diversity, we can discover new things to enjoy and appreciate. Diego also learned that being proud of his heritage is important, and that true friends will support and respect what makes him unique.

The Lonely Bully

On Saturday, William brought a ball over to his dad and asked, "Hey dad, want to play catch?"

His dad barely looked at him as he walked by and said, "Not right now, buddy. I just got home from work."

William was disappointed, but he knew his dad was tired. He had been working extra hours, even on weekends. William hung his head and waited to watch a movie with his dad, but his dad never came out of his room.

He must have fallen asleep after his shower, William thought as he turned off the TV and went to bed.

The next weekend, William was with his mom. He waited eagerly for her to come home from work. Like his dad, his mom was also working harder than before. She had two jobs, and both were difficult and took up a lot of time.

As she stepped through the front door after work, William excitedly called, "Hi, mom! I made you some dinner." He brought her a bowl of salad, some scrambled eggs, and a big cup of her favorite green tea. It wasn't normally what people had for dinner, but it was all William knew how to make. He was only eleven, after all, and he wanted to show his mom how much he loved her.

William's mother looked at him with tired eyes. She didn't look too excited, only sending a small smile his way. She didn't mean to look unhappy- she was just exhausted. She patted his head and said, "Thank you, honey, but please try not to use up all the ingredients, alright? They're expensive."

She didn't mention how tight her budget had gotten ever since she and William's father got a divorce. But William understood that both his parents had been struggling lately.

"Okay, mom," William said softly.

Without another word, William's mother went to her room and accidentally dozed off, leaving poor William to eat the food he made for her.

Living with divorced parents wasn't easy. At first, it felt like a vacation, spending one week with his dad and the next with his mom. But after a year of doing this, William realized this was his new life. It felt like a vacation, and he always had a bag packed. He thought it was only temporary at first, but after a year of doing it, he realized that this was how his life was going to be from now on.

Over time, he started wondering where his actual home was. For a year now, his mother stayed in one house while his father stayed in another house. They weren't too friendly with each other anymore. They never greeted each other when dropping him off or picking him up. They just stayed in the car. He didn't understand what had happened between them or why things were different now.

He realized that none of his friends had this sort of living arrangement. They still lived in the same house, under one roof, with both their parents. When he went over to Evelyn's house the other day, her parents seemed so happy together! It started to feel like he didn't belong to either of his parents' homes.

At school, his grades started slipping, although, of course, his parents didn't notice. He was usually a bright student, but now he was getting average—or even below average—grades. He missed the days when his parents would care about his grades and push him to study.

One day, when Mr. Turner was returning their science tests, William got upset at his bad grade. Suddenly, he noticed that a boy in his class named Jay looked upset too. When he peaked over his shoulder, he saw that Jay had failed the science test.

"Hey, did you fail, Jay? William shouted, loud enough for the rest of the class to hear. Jay looked shocked and immediately pulled the hood of his sweater over his head as the other kids started whispering about him.

Instantly, William felt a lot better about his grade. *At least my grade isn't as bad as Jay's*, he thought to himself with a chuckle. He didn't think about how his words had hurt Jay. He only cared about making himself feel better.

During lunch the next day, William wanted to ask about the science homework that was due for the next lesson. He didn't finish the assignment, and the last thing he wanted to do was to copy someone else's homework. He knew copying was wrong. His mom had told him that if he didn't understand the homework, he should ask a friend or teacher for help instead of cheating.

"If you don't know how to do the assignment, you can ask your friends or teachers to help. But never copy the answers, William. If you do, you won't learn anything. You'll just end up cheating yourself out of a good education.

William put the advice out of his head. He called out to his friend Poppy but she didn't hear him over the hustle and bustle in the cafeteria. She kept walking while talking to her friend, Evelyn.

William knew that Poppy wasn't ignoring him on purpose but he got upset anyway. He remembered the times at home when his parents wouldn't give him the attention he wanted because of how tired they were. He didn't want to be ignored at school too. Angry, he stomped over to Poppy.

Stomp, stomp, stomp!

When he got close enough, he called her name again. This time, Poppy turned around with a big smile.

"Hi, William—" she started to say, but William yanked her hair.

"Ouch!" Poppy cried. William frowned at her.

"That's for not answering me when I called you the first time," he said in a frightening tone. He towered over Poppy, making her look like a tiny mouse next to him.

"I turned around as soon as I heard you, William!" Poppy said angrily, tears in her eyes as she rubbed the spot where he pulled her hair.

"Don't look at me like that!" William suddenly shouted.

Everyone in the cafeteria froze. They were surprised. His classmates had noticed that William had been changing lately, and not for the better. He had grown meaner and started showing less and less kindness towards his friends and classmates.

After that day, everyone was scared of William. No one wanted to play with him during recess, sit next to him in class, or join him at lunch. Even on the bus ride home, kids left the seat next to him empty. And when someone did sit beside him, William would tease or pinch them until they cried.

William was happy with his newfound power. He liked the feeling of being the most powerful kid in class. The only issue was that he became an outcast and started feeling lonely. But he'd finally found a way to release the frustration he felt from the problems he faced at home. He didn't feel good about being a bully, but he felt better overall. He felt strong and powerful, feelings he never felt at home.

One day while everyone was doing some silent reading in the classroom, Mr. Turner came in with a big smile on his face. "Class, eyes on me, please," he called, and all of the kids looked over at him with big, curious eyes.

"Today we have a new friend. Would you like to introduce yourself?" Mr. Turner asked, patting the boy on the back.

The boy's bright smile lit up the entire classroom. He nodded and said, "Hi everyone, I'm Acacius. It's nice to meet all of you--"

"What kind of silly name is that? It sounds like an octopus name!" William burst into laughter. Some kids shook their heads, while others felt bad for the new boy. It was his first day, and William was already giving him a hard time.

"William, that's not nice!" Mr. Turner said sternly.

Acacius simply smiled and explained, "Oh, that's alright. You probably haven't heard it before because it's Greek. I love the meaning behind my name—it means innocent. My father is Greek and my mother is American, so I'm a mix of the two."

William was surprised. Acacius wasn't scared or angry. He just explained calmly with a smile. His positive attitude was contagious, and soon everyone wanted to be friends with him.

During lunch, William decided to pick on Acacius again.

"Hey, worm head!" William called. Acacius turned and laughed. Everyone around him was surprised, but William was the most shocked.

"Oh, you must be talking about my hair. It's curly like my dad's, but I have my mom's blue eyes," he said again with a smile. William couldn't understand why Acacius wasn't afraid of him.

"Aren't you mad that I called you worm head?" William asked, his face turning red like a tomato.

Acacius shook his head. "No, my parents always taught me to be nice to everyone, even to people who are mean. Because we don't know what might be going on in their lives," he said. William froze.

After that, more kids felt brave enough to stand up to William when he was being mean. Acacius had inspired them.

William started thinking about what Acacius had said. It was true—no one knew what was going on at home for him, and he didn't really know what was truly happening in his friend's lives at home.

He thought about all of the terrible things he did to his friends and began to feel really guilty. Slowly, William decided to change his ways. Acacius became his role model. William admired how kind and gentle Acacius was and wanted to be more like him.

One morning, William got to school early and looked for the first two people he had hurt. From a distance, he saw Jay and Poppy talking by the lockers. He walked over quickly.

"Jay? Poppy?" he called nervously.

Jay thought that William was coming over to bully him again and grumbled, "What?"

William gulped.

"I just wanted to say I'm really sorry for teasing you when you failed that test, Jay. And I'm sorry for pulling your hair and yelling at you, Poppy. I know I was wrong, and I'll change," he said. He stared at their shoes and fumbled with his fingers, feeling nervous.

Jay and Poppy were shocked, but when they saw that William was serious, they smiled and said they would forgive him under one condition. They made him promise that he would never bully them again.

And he didn't. William went on to apologize to everyone he had hurt, but he knew that he had to prove that he had changed. So he worked on becoming a much kinder person. William's change of attitude earned him back all the friends he had lost. Over time, he and Acacius even became best friends.

At home, William decided to open up to his parents and tell them how he felt. They felt really bad for how they had been acting and promised to be there for him more.

William realized he had learned the wrong lesson before. Instead of bullying others to feel better and stronger, he should show kindness to build real friendships and support.

William's story teaches us that acting out of frustration and hurting others doesn't solve our problems—it only makes things worse. At first, William thought that being mean made him feel powerful, but he soon realized that it only left him feeling more alone. Through his new friend Acacius, he learned that true strength comes from kindness and understanding. By apologizing to those he hurt and changing his behavior, William found real friendships and the support he needed. This story reminds us that being kind is always the better choice, even when we're going through tough times.

The Shelter Helpers

"And remember, kids. These activities will count towards your mandatory volunteer hours," Mr. Hendrick said while reading the list of names on the paper. His eyes stopped on one name in particular and he looked up at the bright faces of his students.

"Matteo, you're volunteering at the homeless shelter again this week?" Mr. Hendrick asked with a smile.

Matteo nodded. "Yes, sir, with Emily and Ed," he said.

"You've volunteered there five weekends in a row now. You must really love helping at the shelter," Mr. Hendrick said.

It wasn't that Matteo loved it. He just found it was the easiest way to get his volunteer hours done. All Matteo had to do was toss a few ingredients into a big pot and serve it to the homeless. It was usually in the shade, so he didn't have to worry about sweating too much. At the end of every session, the leftover stew would be packed and sent home with the volunteers, which meant Matteo also got a free meal every weekend.

Matteo's mother suggested helping out at an animal shelter, but Matteo was terrified of dogs. His father suggested mentoring, but school was tough enough and Matteo didn't want to spend more time surrounded by books.

On the ride to the homeless shelter, Matteo sat in the backseat with his friends Emily and Ed. They whispered about school, tests, and how they didn't really like volunteering at the shelter.

"It's not the volunteering part that I don't like. It's that we have to help criminals and lazy people," Matteo said loudly enough for everyone in the car to hear. He crossed his arms, annoyed.

"Matteo! We do *not* talk about the homeless that way!" Emily's dad called in surprise and disappointment. "Actually, we don't talk about anyone that way."

"Why not? That's what an old man said last weekend," Emily added, trying to support her friend.

"Which old man?" her dad asked. He kept his eyes on the road but glanced at the kids in the rearview mirror with sad eyes.

"We don't know. He just passed by while we were serving food," Ed said.

"Well, sometimes adults can be wrong. That man was very wrong to say that about those poor homeless people," Emily's dad said firmly, leaving no room for the kids to talk back. "Some people just have it rough in life. That could be any one of us if we're not lucky."

The three children giggled in the back, finding it funny that Emily's father thought they might become homeless one day. Emily's dad sighed and drove the rest of the way in silence.

When they arrived at the shelter, Emily's dad got out of the car and followed the kids inside. They were confused because he usually didn't come with them. They gave him questioning looks, but he just smiled at them and disappeared around the corner.

An hour flew by as Matteo and his friends carelessly threw ingredients into the pot to make some stew. They knew the routine by now and could almost do it with their eyes closed. Then, they served the food and drinks to a long line of homeless people. The adults in charge advised volunteers to serve generous portions.

Just as they were finishing up, Emily's dad called the three of them over. He was standing with some of the homeless people who were clinging on to hot bowls of stew and cold juice boxes.

"Kids, meet my lovely new friends: Pam, Roger, and Janice. They've kindly agreed to share their stories and experiences with us," Emily's dad said. Then he gestured to the three unhappy kids, "And these three are Emily, Matteo, and Ed."

Pam was an old woman. Her hair had turned completely gray and she was hunched over. In her trembling hand was a wooden cane that she used as a walking stick. She had almost no teeth left and her face was mostly wrinkled. But her smile was bright and beautiful.

Roger looked a bit younger, maybe around Matteo's father's age. He had a thick beard and tired, sunken eyes. His clothes were torn in places and his teeth were rotting. He had a long scar on his arm that looked painful. He smiled at the kids but it didn't quite reach his eyes.

Lastly, Janice looked a lot younger. She might have been fresh out of high school. She had a frightened look in her eyes that didn't seem to ever go away. Her long, brown hair was tangled and messy. When the kids looked closer, they saw her hair was also stiff and greasy. She was extremely thin and pale as a ghost.

"Lovely to meet you kids," Pam smiled. The kids gave her shy smiles in return.

"Come closer, kids, and I'll tell you how I became homeless," Pam said. They all gathered around as she started her story. "Just a few years ago, I lived in a big house with my daughter Avery, her husband, and my two little grandchildren. My life was perfect except for some small arguments with my daughter," she said with a sad smile.

"Then one night, on my birthday, Avery told me her husband didn't like me living with them anymore. They had thought I was only staying for a little while. No one had told me this," Pam explained, her eyes filling with tears. "They eventually kicked me out of the house, and with nowhere to go, I ended up living on the streets."

Emily and Ed gasped, but Matteo was confused and upset. He had lost his grandparents years ago and missed them a lot. He couldn't imagine treating his parents like that – he loved them so much.

Then Roger shared his story. He had worked really hard to start his own business, but a flood ruined everything. After that, it became impossible to rebuild the business. He started falling behind on his bills and rent.

"My family and friends loaned me some money a few times, but they couldn't do it forever. Things got worse, and soon I was thrown out of my home without a dime to my name and forced to live in the streets."

Matteo felt shocked. There were so many questions in his head, but he pushed them aside for now.

Janice's story was also sad. She had been sent to juvenile prison for stealing, but no one knew the truth. "I stole food from a store to feed my little brother and sister," she explained. "Our parents died in a car crash when I was seventeen, and our aunt, who was supposed to take care of us, didn't want us around. She was a drug addict and rarely fed us."

"But they don't know that what I stole was food from the store to feed my little brother and sister. Both my parents died in a car crash when I was seventeen and our aunt was supposed to look after us, but she didn't want us around. She was a drug addict and rarely had food for us."

She went on to explain how she wasn't allowed back into her aunt's house because her aunt saw her as a thief, and so she was forced onto the streets.

"It's sad because I used to be an excellent student when I was in school. My dream was to become a doctor, but there's no chance of that happening right now," Janice said.

Matteo thought for a moment and then asked, "Why don't you just get jobs? Wouldn't that help?"

Janice sighed. "It's really hard to get a job when you've been to jail. People don't listen to your story. Once they see a criminal record, they won't hire you."

"No one wants to hire a woman my age, dear. We just have to find ways to get by," Pam said in her crackly old voice.

Pam explained that most of the time, "getting by" meant trying to sell or exchange something for food or begging for spare change.

Then Roger added, "Besides, when you go in for a job interview you need clean work clothes, a permanent address, a phone number... it's difficult for us to have those things. Even basic jobs think twice about hiring homeless people. So we try to work in any way we can to get the money."

The kids listened to some other stories as well about how difficult it was to get medicine, how they were always hungry, not knowing when the next meal was going to come, and shivering while sleeping on the cold hard ground at night.

Emily was crying after hearing their stories, while Ed and Matteo were sniffling. Matteo couldn't believe just how cruel the world could be.

The ride home was quiet while everyone thought about the stories they had just heard. Emily's dad finally broke the silence.

"So Matteo, do you still think that the homeless are just lazy criminals?" he asked.

Matteo hung his head in shame, regretting ever saying such an awful thing. "No, they've been through so much, and we should help them as much as we can," he replied.

That day, Matteo decided he wanted to volunteer more, not just to finish his hours, but to help people. Emily and Ed were also eager to make a change, even if it was a small one.

Back at school, Matteo spoke to his teacher about wanting to create more awareness homelessness, and Mr. Hendrick was more than happy to help. Mr. Hendrick decided that the following weekend, the entire class would take a trip to the homeless shelter to volunteer.

Other teachers also began talking about homelessness and why people might end up without a home. They discussed what the kids in their classes could do to help.

On Friday, the day before the class trip to the homeless shelter, Mr. Hendrick called on Matteo to share his experiences while volunteering and asked what jobs the kids would be expected to do at the shelter, and if they could bring anything to donate.

They created a list of items people could donate. Many blankets, jackets, coats, shoes, socks, and other clothes were donated. Some parents even donated money. Lucy's father, who was a wealthy business owner, arranged for food and hygiene products to be donated as well.

Matteo felt truly thankful for all the blessings in his life—plenty of food, a warm home, and a caring family. Talking to the homeless people at the shelter made him realize they were doing their best with the tough situations they were facing. They deserved to be treated with kindness, not judgment. He felt compassion for those less fortunate and knew he wanted to help in any way he could.

> *Matteo's story teaches us not to judge others based on appearances or assumptions. At first, he thought the homeless were lazy or didn't want to help themselves, but after hearing their stories, he realized that many people face challenges that are hard to imagine. Matteo learned the importance of kindness, compassion, and helping those in need. This story reminds us that everyone deserves to be treated with respect and understanding, and that even small acts of kindness can make a big difference.*

The Unkind Leader

"Alright then, so we all agree that Kai should be team captain?" Miss Amelia, the debate teacher, asked.

Everyone nodded happily. Kai was the best debater on the team, and his teammates thought it made sense for him to be captain.

"This is going to be so much fun, Kai!" Evelyn clapped happily. Their other teammates, Jason, Missy, and Howard, agreed. Everyone was giggling and talking amongst themselves.

Kai felt that he was suited to be captain, too. For the past eleven years, his mother always said that he walked around with a book in his hand—even before he could read. Kai read so much that he was certain he knew nearly everything there was to know.

As his teammates discussed how fun it was going to be to practice together, Kai frowned. He snorted and said, "Debate isn't supposed to be *fun*. It's serious business and we need to practice really hard if we're going to win."

"Oh, of course, we'll practice hard, Kai," Missy said, looking confused. "But we can still have fun too, can't we?"

Kai crossed his arms. "No, I don't think it should be fun at all. I'm team captain now and I say we practice seriously. No more giggling, laughing, and fooling around," Kai announced sternly.

His friends were surprised by Kai's attitude. Normally, he was fun and easygoing, but today, he seemed strict. They didn't argue with him, thinking maybe he was just having a bad day.

Practice went on, but was dull without the usual laughter and fun. The team worked hard, but something was missing. After practice, Kai rushed home, eager to share the news with his parents.

"Mom! Dad!" he called as he burst through the front door.

His parents peeked their heads out from the living room. "What is it, honey?" his mom asked.

"I'm the new debate team captain! Can you believe it?" He cheered and went on to tell his parents about the voting and how he created a new rule about practice being more serious. He stood proudly and his parents looked at each other before smiling down at Kai.

"That's wonderful, sweetie!" his mom said, giving him a big hug. "We're so proud of you."

"Great work, buddy!" his dad added with a grin. "Just make sure you don't let all that power go to your head. Being a good captain means being kind and helping your team."

Kai didn't really understand what his dad meant but nodded anyway. He was just excited to be the leader.

The next day, practice came again, but it wasn't as fun as usual because of Kai's new rule. Miss Amelia noticed how boring it was and tried to get the kids to talk about fun things. But Kai stopped it right away.

"No, Miss," he said. "We can't play around if we want to win."

Miss Amelia frowned. "You can still win while having fun, Kai. Fun doesn't equal to failure," she tried to tell him, but Kai didn't change his mind. So, practice continued the way Kai wanted it.

The regional debate finals were just around the corner and the team decided to have a quick session to discuss potential topics they should focus on.

"I saw an interesting one about whether or not school uniforms should be banned," Howard suggested.

"No, it's not going to be something as simple as that," Kai objected.

Jason spoke up next. "How about if mobile phones should be allowed in classrooms?"

Kai shook his head again.

"Okay, what about the pros and cons of social media for students?" Evelyn asked.

Again, Kai turned the idea down with a big frown on his face. He felt like the topics were too simple and not worth practicing. So the team went on listing off what seemed like perfectly good topics, yet none were good enough for Kai. He simply shook his head and rejected each and every one.

"It's like you guys aren't even trying. Can't you think of anything a bit more difficult? I don't want to practice on baby topics," Kai rudely said as he crossed his arms over his chest.

Jason was starting to get tired of Kai's behavior. He stood up and slammed his hands on the table once Miss Amelia left the room.

"I don't know what's gotten into you, Kai, but you need to stop acting so bossy," Jason said, his face red with anger.

Kai was surprised by Jason's outburst, but he didn't want to back down. "I'm the captain, like it or not. So you have to listen to me, and I said to think of harder topics to practice."

"Why don't you come up with some, then?" Missy asked, also annoyed but trying to stay calm. "We've been giving all the ideas, and you just keep saying no. So why don't you help us?"

"*I* don't have to suggest anything because *I'm* the captain," Kai said again. Kai said loudly. He walked up to the board and started writing everyone's names in columns. When he finished, he turned to face them. "Since I'm the captain, you have to listen to me."

"I'm giving everyone in this room one day to come up with creative topics that we can practice. Otherwise, I'll be forced to kick you off the team," Kai said. He was trying to appear stern and strict, like their principal who wore his glasses at the tip of his nose. But his friends weren't scared at all. They just felt upset with how Kai was acting and didn't want to be around him anymore.

No one spoke. Jason grabbed his bag and stormed out of the room. Soon, everyone else followed.

Kai was really mad. He called for them to come back, but they ignored him. Right before leaving, Evelyn turned and said, "We picked you as captain, but you're treating us really badly. Friends don't do that."

Kai stared at her through his thick-rimmed glasses. He huffed and said, "In here, I'm not your friend. I'm your captain, and you have to do what the captain says if you want to win."

Evelyn tried to reason with Kai, but he wouldn't listen. So, she walked out too. Kai was about to shout about telling Miss Amelia that everyone skipped practice, but before he could, the teacher came back in. She had overheard the conversation and asked Kai to sit down. Kai sat, ready to complain about the whole team. But Miss Amelia spoke first.

"Kai, do you like being the captain?" she asked. Kai nodded excitedly.

"The only thing I don't like is that my teammates are stubborn. They don't listen to me. I'm just trying to get them in the right mindset," Kai said, letting out a sigh.

"And what mindset is that?" Miss Amelia asked, raising an eyebrow.

Kai sat up straight, feeling confident. "A winner's mindset! I can't have them goofing around or practicing on easy topics. Anyone can do that! If we want to win, we have to be different," he said proudly.

Miss Amelia nodded, thinking about what he said. "But wouldn't it be better to practice something, anything, together? Look at today. You argued with the team, and now no one practiced at all."

Kai knew what Miss Amelia meant, but he still thought his way was right.

The next day, the team met again, but things felt tense. No one was talking to Kai. They ignored him and chatted among themselves. Kai got frustrated and went to Miss Amelia to complain. The teacher came over and asked the group to start practicing a topic.

Immediately, they picked a topic one of them had suggested the day before and excluded Kai from the practice session. Kai got mad again and shouted that he was the captain and they had to listen to him. The team continued to ignore him, kept happening every day until the day of the competition. Kai practiced alone, refusing to join the others.

On the day of the competition, Miss Amelia was worried. The team wasn't working together at all. They practiced separately, and it was clear their teamwork was falling apart.

"Don't worry, Miss. I'll win this, with or without them," Kai said confidently.

Miss Amelia frowned. "This is a team effort, Kai. You can't win alone," she said. She was disappointed that Kai still didn't understand the importance of teamwork.

The competition began with a screech over the loudspeaker followed by an announcement.

"Next up, Lake West Elementary versus Willowbrook Elementary. Debaters take your positions," the chairperson announced.

"Willowbrook, you're taking the negative side," the chairperson told Kai, Evelyn, and Jason, while Missy and Howard stood on the side as reserves.

"Okay, so we're arguing against the topic. Got it?" Kai said in a mocking tone.

"We know how this works, Kai," Jason whispered, annoyed. "We're on the debate team too." Evelyn ignored them as she set up her notebook.

"Your topic is... the ban of school uniforms. Lake West will argue for the ban, and Willowbrook will argue against it," the chairperson reminded them.

Evelyn glared at Kai. This was the exact topic Howard had suggested during practice, but Kai had said it was too easy.

As the other team spoke, Kai, Evelyn, and Jason wrote down their notes. But they didn't talk about who would say what. Kai stubbornly waited for his turn to speak. He didn't want to help his teammates since they didn't listen to him.

"Willowbrook Elementary, first speaker," the chairperson spoke.

Kai stood up, adjusted the microphone, and made his point that school uniforms shouldn't be banned because they create unity and equality.

Jason, the second speaker, started to panic. His point was the same as Kai's, and now he had nothing to say. He tried to think of something new, but his mind went blank.

Evelyn realized Jason was panicking but couldn't help him, as he had already stood up and walked to the podium.

Jason's entire body shook with fear and sweat dripped down his face. He brought his mouth to the microphone and he still had no idea what to say. The only thing he muttered was, "Uh..." before sitting back down, completely stuck.

Willowbrook lost the debate, and the ride back to school was filled with arguing.

"It's Jason's fault! He froze and didn't say anything!" Kai yelled.

"No! It's Kai's fault for not letting us practice at all," Evelyn shouted.

Missy jumped into the conversation. "It's all your faults for not working together. You're all selfish and childish!" she cried.

The fighting immediately stopped. Everyone went quiet. They all started thinking about their part in the loss. Kai knew it was mostly his fault. He had been so bossy and power hungry that he had completely ignored what was most important: valuing and respecting his friends' ideas.

"I'm sorry," Kai suddenly said. Everyone looked at him. "I'm sorry for not listening and for misusing my power. I was just really excited."

The team wasn't sure if they should forgive him after how he had acted. Miss Amelia stepped in.

"I think you can trust Kai to change," she said. Then she turned to him, "You need to learn to be a better captain, Kai."

Kai looked up at her, "How can I do that?"

Miss Amelia smiled. "Start by listening to everyone's ideas. A good leader is a good listener. You also need to explain why you're making decisions. Also, a good captain needs think about what's best for the team."

The next day, the team practiced for the next competition. Kai followed Miss Amelia's advice. He listened to his teammates and worked together with them. His friends started to trust him again. They were happy to have Kai as their captain, now that he was working with them and not bossing them around.

Kai learned an important lesson: a good leader builds up their team, while a bad one tears it apart. From that moment on, he vowed to always be the kind of leader who listens, supports, and helps his team succeed.

> *Kai's story teaches us that leadership isn't just about being in charge; it's about listening to others and working together as a team. At first, Kai thought that being strict and controlling would help his team win, but he soon realized that without listening to his teammates, they couldn't succeed. By learning to respect their ideas and collaborate, Kai became a better leader, and his team started to trust him again. This shows that real leadership is about bringing people together, supporting them, and making sure everyone feels valued.*

The Video Game Glitch

Henry Nguyen was a really good gamer for someone who was only twelve. He started playing video games with his older sister, Leah, when he was eight years old.

His parents didn't mind him playing games because Henry was great at managing his time. He always did well in school, helped out around the house, and got all his chores done. He was kind to everyone too.

However, Henry often tried to take shortcuts instead of doing things the proper way.

For example, when he had math homework, he used a calculator to finish quickly. But because he didn't show his work, the teacher gave him a warning and took away some points from his grade.

Another time, his dad found him wearing two pairs of jeans—one over the other! Henry wobbled around like a panda and could barely eat, but he claimed it was faster than wasting time changing out of his outside clothes once they got home.

Henry was a nice kid but often did silly things. His parents, friends, and teachers were used to it.

One day, while Henry was playing Fortnite—his favorite video game—he realized he was doing much better than his teammates. After the game, other players praised him and suggested he should try to play in tournaments.

Henry hadn't thought about that before, but it sounded like a good idea. So, he practiced as much as he could and watched videos of top players to learn new tricks.

His parents were very supportive of him.

"I know you're an incredible player, and it would be great for you to play with other top gamers. But don't forget to have fun—after all, it's just a game," his mother would often remind him.

"Alright, mom, I'll remember that," Henry always said.

One day, Henry rushed downstairs, sweaty and excited. "Mom! Dad!" he shouted.

His parents hurried over, worried something was wrong. "What happened?" his dad asked.

"I qualified! I'm one of the finalists for the Fortnite tournament!" Henry cheered, hugging his parents.

They laughed in relief. "Congratulations, buddy!"

That night, his mom made Henry's favorite meal for dinner—burgers, curly fries, and his favorite chocolate drink, Yoo-hoo. . His sister, Leah, even got him some pizza on her way home from her part-time job. Things couldn't have been going any better for Henry.

A week later, all the tournament finalists met over a video call. Henry was excited to meet other gamers besides his sister. The other finalists were friendly and kind. They all got along so well that they promised each other that no matter who won, they would stay friends and play together after the tournament ended.

The tournament was still months away, and Henry spent all his free time practicing. But as the tournament got closer, he started feeling nervous. Everyone at school knew about it and was cheering him on.

"Good luck, Henry!" Peter shouted after school.

"Make sure you win!" Isaiah said with a big smile.

Even his neighbor congratulated him, saying it was exciting that he had made it so far.

But Henry started worrying—what if he didn't win? Would everyone be disappointed in him? Would they stop being friendly? Would they stop believing in him? He wasn't sure, but it made him feel stressed.

Soon, playing Fortnite didn't feel fun anymore. It felt like hard work. Practicing felt more like a job, and watching videos of pro players felt like a school assignment.

I can't wait for the tournament to be over, Henry thought as he buried his head in his hands.

He was stressed but didn't want to worry his parents or friends, so he always put on a happy face. He knew keeping secrets wasn't right, but he wasn't sure what else to do.

One day, while reading about Fortnite strategies, he stumbled upon something surprising—a cheat code. It was a shortcut that would give him an unfair advantage by keeping his health full no matter what. With the competition just a week away, Henry felt more confident, thinking there was no way he could lose now. He had a secret weapon.

On the day of the tournament, Henry arrived at the hall with his family cheering him on. He played comfortably, not trying too hard because he knew he couldn't lose with his secret trick. But as he kept winning, his opponents grew suspicious.

After winning every single game back-to-back, Henry was beaming with pride. He cheered for himself, feeling on top of the world. He rushed over to meet his new friends—who had been his opponents during the tournament—eager to celebrate with them.

"Did you see that? I won!" he said proudly.

His friends just frowned at him. Henry thought it was strange that they didn't congratulate him. They were usually very supportive and had made a promise to remain friends even after the tournament.

"What's wrong?" he asked.

At first, the group remained silent. Instead of cheering, his friends just frowned. Alice spoke up. "We know you cheated, Henry. There's no way your health didn't go down at all after getting hit so many times."

Henry's heart sank. He hadn't expected to get caught, and now he was filled with panic. What could he say? If he admitted to cheating, he'd be disqualified, and all his hard work would go to waste. Confused and ashamed, Henry slowly walked away from his friends, guilt washing over him.

He knew he couldn't keep it from his parents any longer.

"I have something to tell you," he said nervously when he found them. He bit his lip, trying to hold back his nerves. Despite his stuttering, he finally blurted out the whole story.

His parents and sister listened quietly. He could see the disappointment in their faces, and it made him feel even worse. He started to cry.

His mother pulled him into a hug. "Oh, sweetheart, I'm so sorry we didn't notice how stressed you were," she said softly.

"We were so caught up in the excitement of the tournament that we forgot to check if you were doing okay. We're sorry, buddy," his father added.

His sister Leah, who was also a gamer, understood how hard it was to admit when you did something wrong and face losing an achievement. But she knew Henry had to make things right.

After explaining why honesty and having fun while gaming were important, she said, "I think you know what you need to do, Henry." Leah smiled warmly at him.

Henry nodded and decided to fix the mess he had caused as well as try to mend his friendship. He headed straight to the judges' stand and explained nervously.

Henry nodded and decided to fix the mess he had caused. He headed straight to the judges' stand, feeling nervous but determined.

"Hi, I'm Henry. I won the Fortnite tournament, but I need to admit something." The judges listened carefully. Henry gulped and continued, "I used a cheat code to win."

The judges were shocked but had no choice—they disqualified him. Though it hurt to lose the champion title, Henry knew he had done the right thing.

"I'm really sorry for everything," he said. "You're right, I used a cheat code, and it wasn't fair. I'll never do it again."

"We appreciate the apology," Alice said sadly, "but you did take a spot one of us deserved."

Henry looked at her shyly and replied, "Actually, I told the judges I cheated. You're the real winner, Alice. I've been disqualified."

Alice was stunned. "Wow, I didn't expect that. Thank you, Henry!" She gave him a big hug.

Henry realized that cheating wasn't worth the trouble that followed, and it was much better to play a fair game and lose than to cheat and win.

Henry realized that cheating wasn't worth the trouble. It was far better to play fair and lose than to cheat and win. From that day on, Henry played games honestly and had more fun. He might have lost the tournament, but he won back the trust and respect of his friends—and for Henry, that was the biggest win of all.

Henry's story teaches us the importance of honesty and the consequences of taking shortcuts. While Henry was talented and passionate about gaming, he learned that cheating to win only led to guilt and disappointment. By admitting his mistake and making things right, Henry discovered that true success comes from playing fair and enjoying the journey, not just the end result. This story reminds us that strong character and respect from others are more valuable than any victory achieved through dishonesty.

Conclusion

The ten boys we followed in this book each had their own struggles and challenges, but they also had the courage to learn from their mistakes. With the support of their families, friends, and teachers, they became stronger, kinder, and wiser. We all make mistakes—that's how we learn and grow.

Mistakes don't define you—they guide you. Every mistake is a chance to improve and become even better than you were before. Failure is just learning in disguise, and learning makes you stronger.

A bit of advice from me: you'll face challenges in life, but as long as you stay kind, brave, and thoughtful, there's nothing you can't overcome. And when times get tough, remember you don't have to do it alone. Turn to your trusted grown-ups or your close friends. They're always there for you.

You are an incredible person, doing the best you can every day. Always believe that!

Before we go, here's a special message just for you: You are smart, kind, brave, and full of talent. You're doing great things, and there's so much more ahead for you. Always remember how much you're loved and appreciated—so be sure to love yourself just as much! Keep learning, stay kind, and keep being you. See you soon!

Made in United States
Orlando, FL
10 November 2024

53711275R00095